The
Human Nature
of
Organizations

The
Human Nature
of
Organizations

J. DOUGLAS BROWN

Provost and Dean of the Faculty, Emeritus
Princeton University

amacom A Division of
AMERICAN MANAGEMENT ASSOCIATIONS

The author as a Faculty Associate of the
INDUSTRIAL RELATIONS SECTION
of
PRINCETON UNIVERSITY
has been ably assisted by the staff of the
Section in the development of this study.

International standard book number: 0-8144-5350-3
Library of Congress catalog card number: 73-85862

First printing

Foreword

No ATTRIBUTE of civilization has a longer history or is more pervasive today than human organization. The rise and fall as well as the policies and activities of organizations through the centuries are recorded in thousands of books. Our morning newspaper is full of reports of what organizations are doing. But in this welter of information about particular organizations through time there is little insightful analysis or inductive generalization about the common denominator which persists through all these manifestations and events—the phenomenon of human organization as such.

The reasons for the paucity of analysis and generalization about the nature and functioning of human organization as a social entity are many. The mass of undigested material is overwhelming. The diversity of forms appears infinite. The evidence of participant observers is often charged with preconceptions and bias and is little given to portraying the forest rather than the nearby trees. Most of all, a great deal of what occurs within human organization—and often the most significant factors of human motivation, judgment, art, and attitude—are ephemeral, undefined, and unrecorded. Even the social scientist seeking to discover these factors is handicapped by the hard-learned truth that the thing observed is affected by the presence of the observer. The most effective leaders of organizations are too busy as practitioners of a demanding art to keep clinical records analyzing their thoughts, motives, and actions. Even if they tried to keep such records, it would be difficult to put on paper the complex and subtle elements that enter into dealing with people and problems.

The difficulties faced by the social scientist in analyzing human organization should not deter sociologists, social psychologists, and anthropologists from contributing all the knowledge and hunches they can concerning the behavior of organized groups of people. The historian, the political scientist, and the economist, with an interest in the specific causes and effects of group action, can help. But the hazards of academic analysts are that they are usually specialists within a single discipline and, even more, that they have traded off the advantage of intensive and long-continued participation in the leadership of organizations for the privileges of academic isolation.

Despite all the difficulties which beset the student of human organization, the critical role of larger and larger organizations in the world today warrants any reasonable attempt to develop insights or generalizations which may be useful to those often lonely people

who are responsible for their leadership. The justification of the present effort arises from fifty years of
study of industrial relations in a university, in industry, and in government. Included in this period are
twenty-one years as a senior dean and provost of a
complex and growing university, twenty-nine years
of field research and conferences dealing with senior
executives in industry, membership on several boards
of directors and trustees, many administrative and
consulting assignments in government and, most
valuable of all, numberless opportunities for free-
wheeling discussion of the problems of organizational
leadership with chief and other senior executives. This
interplay of participation in and observation of organizations, on the one hand, and the urge of the
scholar to seek valid generalizations, on the other, has
created a long-standing tension. Only now, after some
years of retirement, has the time seemed ripe to ham-
mer out and express in writing the conclusions which
have been tested and retested over half a century.

The completion of this book comes as the Industrial Relations Section at Princeton University
rounds out its first fifty years. Founded with the support of John D. Rockefeller, Jr. in 1922 and, later,
endowed by grants from eighty national corporations
and eight national unions, it has helped government
officials, industrial executives, trade union officers, and
hundreds of professors and students in their attack on
the problems of human relations, in depression and

prosperity and in war and peace. The author, who has profited by the Section's services since 1926, wishes to record his lasting gratitude.

It is my hope that this study will be of interest to all who are generally involved in the ever growing problems of human organization. My particular concern, however, is that this analysis of the role and arts of the *leader* in human organization will be of help to those dedicated and responsible individuals whose decisions affect the lives of millions of Americans.

J. Douglas Brown

Princeton, New Jersey

Contents

I

The Human Nature
of Organizations

AN UNFORTUNATE BY-PRODUCT of the development of
the large-scale organizations needed to implement the
advances in science and technology is the increasing
tendency to extend the impersonal approach of science
and technology to organizations which, regardless of
size, remain essentially human institutions. Science and
technology have provided new knowledge and devices for human organizations to use. But they have
also created great strains and stresses within the ever
larger human organizations needed to put new dis-
coveries to work. Science and technology have not
altered the persistent and controlling attribute of
human organization—namely, whatever the organization's size or form, it continues to be subject to the
complex and unpredictable initiatives and responses of
the individual human beings who make it up. This is
the human nature of organizations.

In science and technology, great progress has been

made in discovering the nature and interactions of nonhuman substances and instruments. Observation, analysis, and experimentation have built up a vast accumulation of knowledge which forms the stable foundation for further advances. This accumulation proceeds generation to generation as a resource distinct from the changing attitudes and emotions of each generation of people. In human organization, however, the attitudes and emotions of each generation of people, developed anew in each maturing person, are the primary influences upon organization, affected but not controlled by inherited knowledge and tradition.

In the world of science and technology, knowledge and the technical skill to put it to work are paramount. In the world of human organization, values, aspirations, emotions, and beliefs saturate the substance of knowledge and reason. Human organization reflects the variable and subjective forces it seeks to contain for the attainment of its purpose. There is grave danger in confusing the two worlds or permitting the boundary between them to become vague. The danger is the greater because a clearer understanding of the principles and art of human organization, as distinct from those applicable to science and technology, is needed to bring peace and well-being to the world.

And now, in the greatest acceleration of discovery in the history of the world, science has already blurred our thinking on the complex problems of securing peace and well-being through human organization. To end a war wasteful of lives and the resources of life, we have used ever more efficient instruments of destruction developed by science and technology instead of more vigorously seeking greater understanding of ways to gain cooperation through organization. This encroachment of the world of science upon the world of human affairs is characterized by a misapplication of the analogies from science in dealing with organized human beings. If a greater force overcomes a lesser force, the lesser force is neutralized. We wrongly assume that a member of a human organization, like a known molecule in chemistry, will, with high probability, react in a predictable way to a known external stimulus. If a destructive weapon of a given power causes some degree of fear, a more powerful weapon leads to greater fear, until submission is gained.

But, unlike a molecule in chemistry, the human member of an organization is neither "known" or insensible. Rather, he is a self-conscious, self-initiating individual. He may through fear be led to greater and greater efforts in retaliation against those who seek to intimidate him. A thousand individuals reacting to even a single stimulus, diversely interpreted, react on each other to create a system of responses which make the logical analogies from science both ridiculous and dangerously misleading. A single bomb may paralyze an individual with fright. A continuing deluge of massive bombing may arouse a people to heroic resistance.

When the scientist understands the nature of a

molecule, he is well on his way to understand how a million such molecules will react. The limited understanding we have gained about the reactions of diverse individuals falls desperately short of predicting the behavior of an organization of a million individuals. The hard-won laws, principles, and methods of physical science are a great resource for human progress, but to carry them over by plausible analogy to the behavior of human organizations is neither scientific nor helpful.

Paralleling the advance of science and technology has been the enormous growth of political, economic, and social organizations which seek to direct human affairs. With great size, the influence of the individual appears to diminish. The organization, because of its mass and its internal cohesion, appears to attain a personality and momentum of its own. It becomes easy to think of the organization in monolithic terms, as if it were no longer a combination of human beings but rather a separate entity following self-determined, pseudophysical principles. The subtle shift appears not only in common speech such as in discussing "General Motors," "the Defense Department," or the "Catholic Church" as if they were monolithic structures, but also in the more sophisticated studies of the social scientist. This easy shorthand of speech unfortunately betrays a conceptual confusion of bigness with internal integration. That human organizations require some degree of tradition and "momentum" is unquestionably true. But that this justifies the transfer of the approach of the physical sciences to the study of their behavior involves a basic misunderstanding of their essential nature. The initiating forces which control the behavior of an organization remain human and disparate even under the greatest pressures for cohesion and conformity. Human organizations persist in being human. Dictators have learned this to their sorrow.

The great advances which have been made in statistical recording and analysis of *past* data in political, economic, and social activities may suggest that this has become the entering wedge of science in the handling of human organizations. The point must be immediately emphasized, however, that while sophisticated statistical analysis uses mathematical procedures in manipulating quantifiable data on *past* experience, it in no way creates any scientific "predictability" not inherent in the raw material upon which it is based. If people change their minds or their habits, a mathematical formula will not help foretell the change. Although historical data may be helpful in itself as a guide to decision, any predictions concerning the *future* behavior of people remain subjective judgments quite distinct from the application of the highly predictive laws of physical science developed to deal with nonhuman substances.

Despite the expanding use of computers and mathematical procedures, we are still unable to predict from past evidence the swings of political attitudes, business enterprise, consumer spending, birth rates, or fashions before change has already begun. We are but recording change, not predicting it. We can develop extensive analyses of past attitudes and behavior, but because of the diverse impacts of a multitude of influences upon a multitude of diverse people, wise prediction is far more the result of mature understanding, sensitive intuition, and considered judgment than of the scientific marshaling of historical, quantitative evidence. One does not have to try to predict the fluctuations on the New York Stock Exchange indices to learn this.

Far from being a cause for discouragement, the essential need for human understanding, intuition, and judgment in the planning of human affairs, in both individual and organized activities, is an inspiring challenge in developing a better world. If human organization followed the pattern of the laws of the physical world of science, the bounds of human progress would be limited by the finite nature of the physical world since its creation. If, however, we accept the premise that human understanding, intuition, and judgment are the primary influences in organized human activity, then we acknowledge that the condition of society in all its aspects is susceptible to the same limitless improvement that is possible in human personality. The world of human organization, translating the vast intangibles of the human spirit, becomes a world distinct and different from that of science with its subjection to persistent, nonhuman determinants.

Mature judgment based on observed experience

involves attributes of patience, understanding, and tested insight not readily available to younger men. It is not easy for the student of human organization to pull himself away from the strong attractions of the scientific methodology of the mathematically based sciences. The marshaling of elaborate quantitative data, abstracted from available sources and analyzed by sophisticated mathematical procedures, affords a sense of security in the neatness of the results. That these techniques mean a reduction in the number of variables to those readily quantifiable and the assumption that thousands of individuals, despite new and diverse influences, will again act as they did in the past, is pushed into the background in the excitement of an "objective" analysis. To shun this attractive exercise and to use instead the inductive process of resolving human experience into loose and tentative patterns of group behavior seems "unscientific."

But as one gets older, the shortcomings of quantitative methods become more evident. The personally observed history of human organizations in action, buttressed by the numberless episodes of recorded history, give one faith that judgment and insight gained from *qualitative* evidence can be more useful than *quantitative* exercises in contributing to our knowledge of how human organizations work.

The shift in emphasis from scientific prediction based on quantifiable evidence to judgment based on qualitative evidence in dealing with human organization may appear to some to be a backward step in an age of science and technology. For centuries there has been a growing tendency—among those awed by scientific discovery—to believe that "proof" through the manipulation of measurable data is the only means of attaining truth. But even in respect to the physical world this belief is based on a partial and vague understanding of the nature of scientific discovery. It disregards the subjective nature of many of the steps along the way as well as the very nature of truth itself.

The subjective, nonquantifiable elements in the total process of scientific discovery are far more significant than is realized by those who would attempt to tranfer the methods of physical science to the analysis of human organization. The creative ideas which have pushed forward the frontiers of scientific knowledge have been largely the result of human intuition based upon an intermingled and interacting combination of qualitative and quantitative evidence. The intuitive processes of the human mind have vastly greater range and flexibility than any computer. Mathematics itself is a highly subjective activity of the human mind. The interpretation of data and its relevancy to the proof sought involves both the presuppositions and the judgments of the scientist. These are, in turn, influenced by the general state of knowledge relevant to his field. And finally the proof attained, even though tested by elaborate quantitative procedures, remains but a prediction, a probability which, because of the elegance, symmetry, neatness, and fit of the elucidation is called "truth."

It is probably not scientific discovery but rather the technological applications of science which have been the major cause of exaggerating the contributions of "science" to the study of human organization. Overlooked is the fact that technology implements but a small and well-tested fraction of the scientific knowledge available at any given time. Again, there are great demands upon human understanding, intuition, and judgment to determine which scientific findings are applicable, useful, and economic in any new device. The time lag of application may be years or centuries. The complications of coordinating diverse elements into design or operation may be almost unmanageable, and the costs may far exceed the gain in efficiency. The history of technology is full of examples of the many problems of converting scientific knowledge into effective machines. The development of power from steam to atomic fusion, the history of automotive transportation by land and air, and the problems of forecasting or controlling weather conditions are but samples of the vast and often frustrating complexities which technology must deal with to implement scientific knowledge.

But the layman may still ask, "If science and technology can get men to the moon and back, why can't they help us design an effective human organization?" The answer may become clearer if, for purposes of comparison, the machine which takes men to the moon were considered to be a system of ten thousand parts each designed on the basis of accumulated knowledge and skill gained through centuries and combined into a most complex, interacting mechanism. Each part is built to precise specifications and is intended, so far as possible, to perform a precise function at the command of human beings, directly or indirectly, through a train of interlocking devices. The more perfect the machine, the more completely it performs the commands of the operators without question, inattention, or resistance. The determination of purpose remains a human function.

Compare such a beautiful mechanism with a human organization of ten thousand members. No matter what effort has been expended to attain machinelike operation at the direction of some master operator, a human organization remains fundamentally different from a machine both in its constituent parts and in the way it functions. The members have *not* been designed on the basis of scientific or technological knowledge to fulfill the specific purposes of a human operator. Rather they have evolved as infinitely complex, distinct personalities, each with emotions, aspirations, intelligence, and incentives in unique combination. Communication with each member and between members at all levels is not mechanically precise, but is saturated with conscious and unconscious subjective interpretation. Response to direction stems not from the feedback of an interlocked mechanism but from ten thousand separate foci of initiative and motivation. Each individual's response is affected by his changing reaction to not only immediate, external stimuli from all possible sources but also to internal stimuli arising from conscious thought or emotions or unconscious suggestion which are the result of his total life experience.

Here is the point where the scientist-statistician makes a bold assumption based on the laws of probability developed in dealing with objective, physical phenomena. The assumption is that, although the actions of individuals may be unpredictable, those of a large number of individuals can be predicted. Overlooked is the fact that people, unlike molecules, are conscious, self-determining personalities which are distinct points of initiative and response. Further, they are influenced in their initiative and response by each other in a highly complex system of intercommunication that ranges over the whole gamut of human transmission of attitude, thought, and emotion. Because of the *human* nature of the constituent elements of a body of people, the unpredictability of one person's response carries over to the unpredictability of the response of a large number of people wherever freedom of action or thought exists. Under some conditions, group behavior may reflect the clash of heterogeneous attitudes and tendencies of individuals; under other conditions, because of compensatory balancing, it may not. The important fact is that the result of group interaction is unpredictable in contrast to the behavior of nonhuman materials. This is why we must avoid the easy transfer of the methods of physical science to the study of human organization, which is a far more complex and subtle area of understanding.

Human organization, to be truly constructive, must coordinate the activity of individuals acting as self-conscious, self-determining persons. The useful work of the world requires such organization. The extent to which individuals can be organized into effective human structures and not into machines, mobs, or herds of animals will be determined by how well we can come to understand the difference between human organizations and machines, mobs, or herds of animals.

One very subtle way to depersonalize human organization is to discount the degree to which *some* members of an organization can or should act as self-conscious, self-determining persons. Their behavior is circumscribed, it is claimed, not by objective, physically definable forces, but rather because they are or should be controlled by *socially* determined, not *individually* determined, goals. This approach does not deny the human nature of organization, but shifts the center of self-conscious determination and initiative from *all* members of the organization to some higher order of human beings that seeks to enforce a set of socially established standards. This form of depersonalization, which strikes some segments of a society and not others, is important in our analysis because of its widespread occurrence and also because of its adverse consequences.

In the long history of human society, the segmented depersonalization of human organization has taken many forms. The limiting case is that of a society in which some members are abject slaves entirely subject to the will of their masters. From earliest times, members of a tribe have been subject to established customs in which age-old anxieties and superstitions were inextricably merged with an effective way of life. These customs not only controlled to varying degrees the actions of individuals, but their values and attitudes as well. Through the ages, leaders of organized societies, whether warrior chiefs, anointed kings, or priests claiming supernatural inspiration, have assumed authority over the individual to direct his actions and to impose a system of values upon his mind and conscience. The divine right of kings was a more recent and more sophisticated application of the concept. In our own day, the right assumed by a dictator or a dictatorial oligarchy to determine the thought as well as the actions of individuals is an attempt to depersonalize human organization by the elimination of the self-conscious determination of the individual.

But there are more subtle ways in which the depersonalization of human organization has occurred. A *society* may, like a primitive savage who fears a supernatural god, come to assume the existence of some source of values or some determinant in social change which is impersonal, whether benign or evil. It is not some powerful group in society which establishes such values or initiates such change, even though they may take advantage of them. Nor is it the functioning of an inhuman, machinelike mechanism. Rather it is society itself, as a cohesive, disparate entity, which is assumed to be the causal agent.

An example of this kind of depersonalization is the widespread acceptance of Adam Smith's premise that, under a policy of laissez faire in England at the time of the Industrial Revolution, ruthless competition among enterprisers in some mysterious way led to social benefit, a higher value, despite the resulting hardship for millions of workers. By the workings of an "unseen hand," a "social value" existed apart from the value judgments of individuals. That this was not merely the theory of a social philosopher but, as time passed, a factor in the depersonalization of human organization in the English factory system is clearly evident to any reader of history.

Another example of depersonalization by the power of ideas is embodied in Karl Marx's *Das Kapital* and in the influence of this book in spreading the concept that forces in society itself, beyond those controllable by individual, human decision, would bring about violent change. Altered by repeated revision, this concept of a socially determined force arising from values inherent in society itself and not from its constituent individuals has become the philosophic basis of communist ideology throughout the world. Karl Marx's prophecies may not have been borne out, but his derogation of the essential source of values in human organization—the self-conscious, self-determining individual—has affected the political structures of a large part of the world. The fact that a powerful dictator or oligarchy has assumed the prerogative of interpreting and enforcing the appropriate "social values" upon the great majority of citizens does not seem to be recognized as a fundamental departure from Marxian concepts.

Both logic and experience support the conclusion that the values implemented in a society or organization are but the shifting, disparate *relative* evaluations of those who have influence within it. There is no possibility of a separate, definite, and commensurable entity, such as "social value," which can, of itself, control or activate a society or organization. The source of values in a human organization are, therefore, not only human but individual. Individuals, in their evaluations, act upon each other in infinite ways and degrees and over long spans of time. The role of tradition in human organization will be discussed later. For the present, it is important to refute Adam Smith, Karl Marx, and the many others who have over the centuries attempted to shift the focus of initiative in the values which activate human organization from the participating human individuals to some conglomerate, social entity. What influences the *individual* in his value system, whether human or divine, is an entirely different matter. But, as an individual, he is neither a cog in a pseudophysical machine nor a perpetual slave of a man-made social mechanism.

The study of human organization must, therefore, begin with the study of how the individual acts when he is a part of an organization. We want to learn how the acts of many individuals can be best coordinated to attain a desired purpose. The following chapters will seek to help in this endeavor. The conclusions will not, for reasons already discussed, depend upon scientific proof or statistical evidence, but rather upon judgments gained over many years of active participation in and analysis of human organization as a critical instrument in man's survival. Because of his key position, the study will begin with the leader and his role in the organization he seeks to lead.

II

The Attributes of
the Effective Leader

THE MORE FULLY human organization is distinguished
from a machine and recognized as a structured combination of self-conscious, self-determining individuals, the more significant becomes the role of the
leader in human organization. The operator of a
machine manipulates controls designed to assure predetermined, specific performance. The leader of human organization in a free society is charged with the
responsibility of developing a complex and coordinated system of responses from many individual centers of reaction and initiative. The mastery of the
operator over the motions of a machine is so complete
that the term "authority" seems inappropriate. In contrast, the authority of a leader of human organization
is so involved in a complex of interactions that the
term is more applicable to schematic charts than to the
way an organization is actually motivated.

A machine does not react to the personality of the

operator, but rather to his skills. Since the primary job of the leader in human organization is to obtain a response from other human beings, it is axiomatic that these other human beings will react to the leader as a human being and not to his directives alone. It is so much a part of common experience that the response of one person to another's command or suggestion is affected by the overtones of interpersonal reactions that we often overlook the significance of this simple, fundamental fact in the structure of human organization. But it is common knowledge that, over time, neither the status nor the authority of a leader, taken alone, will completely assure a predetermined response. Nor will the logic underlying his directives be clearly distinguished from his total image.

It is interesting to consider the influence of the leader's personality in the most authoritarian of all human organizations—the army in the field. The personal image of great commanders like Alexander the Great, Napoleon, and Robert E. Lee enormously enhanced their effectiveness among their troops. By contrast, in many large American corporations today factors of rapid turnover, divided responsibility, and exaggerated rationality have so beclouded the higher levels that an essential element in effective leadership —a strong personal image—is attenuated and dispersed. If the corporation seeks merely to be a financial holding company, this may be understandable. Our discussion, however, concerns human organizations which strive for effectiveness as integrated, operating structures.

It is a challenging exercise to isolate and define the attributes that are basic to effective leadership. The effort is difficult because the leader must gain response within organizations that differ widely in nature and circumstances. Therefore, it is necessary to distinguish between attributes which are apparently common to all good leaders and those which are variable and supplement the leader's effectiveness more in some situations than in others. It is also evident that there can be no quantitative proof of the significance of any attribute since the attribute is but an intangible element in a complex of such elements in the leader's mode of thought, feeling, and action. The relative importance of a particular attribute is, therefore, a matter of the observer's judgment formed over the years by a sensitive evaluation of both leaders and organizations. The best that any observer can provide is a summary of working premises.

It can be postulated that the common and basic attributes of the effective leader will center on those elements of human personality which affect interpersonal relations. The anonymous transmission of a directive or a fact is not leadership, even though it often passes for such. If human organization is recognized as fundamentally different from a machine, the difference begins at the top and pervades the whole. That difference lies at the point where one person relates to another. If the leader's function is to gain response from people, he must in some way relate to them. There is no person more important in a vast system of interrelations than the one at the top.

It can be argued that in human organization the leader's sensitive understanding of human nature is more vital to his performance than any vast accumulation of knowledge or skills concerning science, technology, statistics, or abstract reasoning. Such human understanding is the outgrowth of deeply subjective elements of personality which have been developed since earliest childhood. Neither accumulated knowledge nor exact reasoning can of themselves produce it. One cannot say that the effective leader of a large organization is born and not made, but, whatever his inherited traits, the molding of them into the capacity for leadership starts very early and, consciously or unconsciously, shapes his way of life.

In a day when chief executives are provided with elaborate staffs to supply data, advice, and service it may seem that this great emphasis upon human understanding, as contrasted with specialized technical capacities, is out of proportion. But the more closely one observes chief executives in action, the more one is impressed by the extent to which human understanding saturates his critical decisions and actions.

The most obvious application of human understanding is in the choice of staff. It also permeates the process of acquiring and evaluating the ideas and judgments of colleagues and staff in day-to-day operations. The ideas and judgments are those of people and cannot be neatly distinguished from their source. Further, the art of motivating people involves the leader's fullest capacities for encouragement and restraint, which must be measured out in each case by an intimate understanding of each individual. Leadership in any organization, regardless of size, operates with people and through people. Decisions based on such clearly quantifiable evidence that they are virtually automatic do not tax a chief executive's capacity for human understanding. But neither are they the important grist of the mill. What most concerns the chief executive is the decision for which there is no clear-cut quantifiable evidence, or for which the available evidence contains hidden elements of personal judgments, especially those concerning the reactions of employees, consumers, competitors, the public, or the government. He is neither a statistician nor an engineer; he is a leader of human beings operating in a world of human beings.

The understanding of human response in a widening spectrum of people is at the core of the chief executive's function. The wise executive always remains aware that human response, in all its manifestations, emanates not from a monolithic, impersonal mass, but from a constantly changing complex of interacting, self-conscious individuals. We Americans, with our fondness for systems and techniques, have tried to measure human response with survey techniques. But as with all statistics, polling surveys have the limitation that they are out of date when completed. Even more, they measure responses that tend to be oversimplified and spontaneous. They fail to reach down into the structured values and attitudes which are of most concern to the organization leader. A statistical survey may help sell soap; it does little to help a leader sense the morale of his organization or to know just how to improve it.

The most valuable guide available to the leader in his efforts to understand human nature is as complete an understanding of himself as he can possibly attain. People who expect leaders to be warm, outgoing extroverts will think it paradoxical that all the great leaders in human history have been introspective. The fact is that a leader consciously or unconsciously tests the response he seeks in others on the anvil of his own mind and emotion. Human response involves such subtle nuances and variables that much is lost in its articulation in conventional terms. But in one's own mind, the conscious and unconscious and the expressible and inexpressible become blended into a working consensus. The leader who has learned to seek this consensus as a support to reasoned judgment whenever human response is involved has gained a precious resource. The advice of others will never replace the sensitive instrument of personal introspection.

The understanding of self which comes with introspection provides the responsible leader with one of the most fundamental attributes of effective leadership—integrity. In the meaning here intended, integrity implies that a person has developed, over time, a consistent ordering of his system of values, attitudes, and goals. In common terms, he has come to know his own mind, conscious and unconscious, and for what he stands and for what he will fight. In the effective leader, this kind of integrity is not alone a moral or intellectual qualification for appointment. It is an attribute functionally prerequisite to continuing effectiveness in directing day-to-day operations in human organization.

It is in the nature of viable organizations that the decisions of the leader or of his higher associates will involve considerations too complex or too little known for a larger constituency to understand. Further, policies or purposes may need to be changed to adjust to new conditions, which may disturb many of the people affected. It appears to be in the nature of human organization that, at such times, the great majority of constituents react to the persistent image of the leader rather than to the precise logic of his decisions. The image of the leader is not his superficial self, but rather the personification of a system of values which he has demonstrated over time. When this manifestation is clear and consistent and reflects a quality of personal integrity, it is a powerful instrument.

In the study of leaders and leadership, one becomes impressed by the difference between the way people respond to the leader of integrity who seizes upon new opportunities and the way they respond to the opportunistic leader who cleverly reacts to new circumstances without testing his decisions against a constant system of personal values. In the short span, members of an organization may admire cleverness. But in the longer life of ongoing organizations, cleverness wears thin in the minds of people who are concerned with the fundamental factors of fairness, foresight, wisdom, and responsibility. These are the elements of leadership which affect them and their future. Such factors in leadership are more understandable to the rank and file because they exist in the whole fabric of human relationships. When one talks among members of an organization about confidence in a leader, it is interesting to see how quickly the emphasis shifts from regard for overt indications of intelligence and skill to concern for a deep-set and consistent system of personal values. Confidence, then, is primarily rooted in a leader's integrity in the larger sense of the term.

Integrity is not a quality derived from logic alone but also from the subtle intuitive processes of the mind. A person may argue with himself that a certain act or policy is justified by all the evidence he can marshal for conscious, rational review. But then, sometimes when this logical exercise is completed, something, drawn from his unconscious self, tells him that the logical conclusion is wrong. This ability to draw intuitively upon one's total experience, of which logical reasoning is only a part, is a precious attribute of leadership, especially in highly responsible positions.

Not only does intuition enhance the quality of judgment but, in organization, it tends to anticipate response. Intuition is a deep and persuasive factor in the reactions and motivation of all human beings. It is often more persuasive than logic, especially when the evidence for logical analysis is limited. It follows that a decision affecting human organization which draws upon both logic *and* intuition, especially where value judgments are involved, is more likely to gain effective response than a decision based on logic alone. It is, therefore, the attribute of *intuitive* integrity that is the precious ingredient in leadership.

As organizations become larger and larger, the integrity of the chief officer becomes more important, not less. This may appear paradoxical to those caught up in the tendency to carry over the analogy of large scale mechanisms to large human organizations. Because a large organization develops an elaborate apparatus of direction and control, supported by research, consultation, statistical and accounting analysis and reports, the apparatus may come to overshadow the human beings who make it viable and effective. If this confuses the general public, it is an understandable error. If it confuses the leader, or those associated with him, it becomes the contagious virus which produces an uninspired, mechanistic bureaucracy.

In the absence of top leadership of integrity, there is no source from which this essentially human quality in leadership will permeate downward through the organization. Integrity, as here defined, cannot be legislated. Nor can it be induced by exhortation. It is carried downward by a long series of person-to-person relationships. The longer the series, the clearer must be the originating signal. There is no more positive distinction between a great machine and an effective human organization than the fact that the engineer *objectively* designs "integrity" into the machine, whereas the leader *subjectively* creates a climate of integrity by his personal attributes, projected downward through organization.

Closely allied with the essential attribute of intuitive integrity in human organization is the sense of total responsibility. In leadership, total responsibility is more than the sum of the parts. In the top position, no job specification can delimit the obligation to weigh all factors, tangible and intangible, measurable and immeasurable, in making any significant decision. Senior officers and committees may bring together much of the material and many of the considerations that go into decisions, but they do not have the unique capacity of the single responsible person to weigh and integrate all possible factors in coming to a decision. In a sense, total responsibility is the positive thrust of the intuitive integrity of the leader. It is the cementing together of the elements of decision into a constructive policy which fits the purposes, standards, and highest potentiality of the organization as seen through the mind of the leader.

In our time the total responsibility of the top leader of a large organization may become impaired by a subtle introduction of administrative technology. In small organizations, the leader who makes ready decisions based on limited evidence is admired. But in modern large organizations, the multiplicity of evidence—from many sources and with elaborate statistical refinement—creates a tendency to assume that the feedback of historical, tangible, quantifiable evidence should determine a leader's decisions. But the executive is not dealing with a machine that moves in response to its own feedback circuits. He is dealing with a human organization with multiple centers of initiative and response. In its most sensitive aspect, responsibility is tested by an acute appreciation of the importance of that response. The leader in even the largest organization cannot default on his obligation to put *his* human understanding into his decisions, no matter how persuasive the "objective" evidence put before him. He must exercise total responsibility himself if he expects this approach to be reflected in his organization. The human organization whose policy reflects an exaggerated regard for statistical feedback becomes an uninspired bureaucracy. It takes more than statistical justification to give human organization the purpose and enthusiasm that lifts it out of machinelike routine.

The counterpart of total responsibility is the courage to sustain it. When all the evidence is in and all appropriate consultation has taken place, the chief executive must put his judgment on the line with conviction and even stubbornness. It is in the nature of human organization that indecision breeds indecision. Subordinates are quick to sense indecision because it is a common human trait. It is excused in oneself, but not in one's leader. Something short of the best possible decision may indeed become the best if it stirs the enthusiasm of the members of the organization and maintains their respect. The best possible decision too long delayed or too tentatively communicated may lead to uncertainty and doubt. The trumpet must give forth a certain sound.

The attributes of human understanding, introspection, intuitive integrity, a sense of total responsibility, courage, and decisiveness might seem to form a complete substructure of personality for the effective leader in human organization. But there remains an attribute that must be present to pull these all together into a dynamic whole. The additional ingredient is a deep and abiding want for accomplishment. The best of leaders find themselves by losing themselves in the accomplishment of their organizations. The task of the leader is persistently demanding and often lonely, and the tangible rewards may be insufficient to sustain his interest and effort. Just as intangible factors cement human organization into a working whole, so the desire for accomplishment brings the leader's underlying qualities into focus in a sustained application of his powers. Without this dynamic ingredient, far fewer men would seek the responsibilities involved in leadership. The sine qua non of those who meet their responsibilities best is the identification of personal accomplishment with that of their organization.

There remains still another basic attribute, one that is difficult to define but is readily recognized in successful leaders. Probably the best term for it is style. Since human beings respond most deeply to other human beings, there should be something in the leader which differentiates him from the crowd and marks him as unique. It is in the nature of style that it does not fit a standardized pattern in human personality but is a variable attribute peculiarly distinct and specific to its possessor. At the same time, whatever it is, it must touch a responsive chord in other people. It may involve a whole gamut of human qualities from what has come to be called charisma to clarity of mind and expression, sustained enthusiasm, sympathy, courage, wisdom, originality, humor, sensitivity, and cultural refinement. However style is expressed, it must be a visible manifestation of a unique personality. An aura of excellence surrounds such a leader, and this tone usually elicits warm approval. Whatever the total personality of the leader may be, some attribute or attributes must have sufficient force to project downward into his organization. The dull efficiency of the machine contains no element of style.

A leader's particular style will not fit all situations. As a highly personal and variable quality, a leader's style may gain effective response in some circumstances and not in others. Organizations have rhythmic patterns of expansion and consolidation, of need to assume new risks and need to prune questionable commitments. Sometimes an organization needs a leader who can create a calm climate of mutual confidence, while at another time there is need for vigorous advocacy of change. Since it is not easy for a leader to change his style, it is usually wise and sometimes necessary to select a leader whose style best fits the special character or prevailing problems of an organization.

The illustrations of style as an attribute of leadership are spread throughout history. In political leadership they are beyond counting. One needs but mention great leaders such as Elizabeth I, George Washington, Abraham Lincoln, Winston Churchill, or Franklin Roosevelt. The great religious leaders of the world have projected a style which still pervades their image in the world. In music, every person who has achieved stature did so largely *because* of his style.

It may seem a long way from these heights to a corporation, a university, or a steel mill, but anyone who has observed leaders in such organizations over time has seen the effect of their style. Whatever other virtues the leader may have, a native attribute of style enhances the tone and depth of response. An organization may continue to function in the absence of style, but without its projection by leadership a catalytic element is missing.

We are not seeking to build a manual for the selection of presidents but rather to examine the nature of human organization, and so for the purposes of our discussion of the human nature of organization, it is not necessary to define the more special qualifications of the leader in relation to a particular assignment. The required amount of knowledge of techniques, technology, processes, or products within the leader's zone of influence may vary widely. Clearly its absence can affect response as well as effectiveness. But a specific amount of knowledge of operations is not in the nature of a basic, common attribute of leadership, and it is a great mistake to assume that such knowledge can substitute for the basic qualities of real leadership already discussed. It is far more important that a leader understand his role, as such, and the arts of leadership in human organization which will be discussed in the next chapter.

III

The Role and Arts
of Leadership

IN THE PRECEDING CHAPTER it was assumed that the
leadership of a unit of organization should be centered in a single individual. The question may be
raised whether organizations today, with large size
and complex problems, have not reached a point
where the focus of leadership should be broadened to
include a group of persons rather than rely upon a
single individual. The feasibility and effectiveness of
such a move can be best considered in relation to the
function and process of leadership in human organization.

Can an organization be effective without the presence at some focal point, or at a hierarchical system
of focal points, of a single person who is more responsible than any others for welding the organization
or a subdivision into a coordinated team? Cannot a
group of intelligent, able, and dedicated persons so
consolidate their understanding, thoughts, and efforts

that they constitute a single focus of executive leadership without permitting any individual within the group to acquire more influence or greater visibility? We are not concerned here with boards of directors or trustees with broad oversight over policy, but rather with the full-time direction of an organization. It reminds one of the old quip that when all men are equal some become more equal than others. Is there an element of wisdom in the quip which is applicable to the way leadership develops in human organization?

A premise based on years of observation is that a group of people joined in an activity which requires coordination instinctively seeks a single individual as the focus of coordination. This appears to be a tendency deep down in the behavior pattern of human beings as well as of many of the higher animals which act in groups. Perhaps it involves an instinct for survival by getting things done, whether obtaining food, defending against aggression, or maintaining order. Egalitarianism is a fundamental concept in the religion, social ethics, or political philosophy of civilizations that respect the innate dignity and political rights of the individual, but in the organized activities intended to preserve and enhance the dignity, rights, and conditions of the individual, the concept of egalitarianism as a philosophical principle gives way to the common acceptance that people are not equal in their capacities to perform *particular* functions, especially that of leadership.

The development of the individual leader in human organization stems from the hierarchical pattern sought by all closed groups. The examples of the tendency to hierarchical relationships in animals are well known. A wolf pack has its leader, and so does a herd of cattle, a pride of lions, or a flock of chickens. The process of finding the leader may involve a long series of shifting interrelationships where one individual challenges all others to establish his rank. In other situations the leader may compete with only a few to attain top status. In human society every conceivable way of attaining and holding leadership is known. Whatever the method and no matter how civilized the conditions, the need for leadership and the hierarchical approach to assuring it remain fundamental to the dynamics of organized endeavor.

The difficulty with group leadership is that it attempts to truncate the hierarchical evolution of leadership short of its final stage. Not only is this abnormal curtailment difficult to bring off, given the human instinct for hierarchy, but it is likely to prove a handicap in the exercise of the leadership function of gaining response. People look to individuals for leadership, not to committees.

Some of the shortcomings of "group leadership" become evident when one attempts to find within the group the attributes of an effective *individual* leader. Although each member of a combined executive board or committee, seeking as such to lead an organization, may possess human understanding, will a joint decision reflect the quality of warmth that one person can communicate? Can there be a common, interlocking sense of intuitive integrity in a group when the source of such integrity must be the introspective thought and feelings of distinct individuals who can intercommunicate these only partially? Responsibility, courage, and a desire for accomplishment can exist in all members of a group, but decisiveness and the sense of *total* responsibility may be dulled by natural differences in experience, attitude, and perception.

The attribute of style is virtually submerged in a group. Style is an essentially personal quality in human beings. It cannot be combined and averaged any more than a group of composers, artists, or architects can combine to design a distinctive masterpiece. Where is the image to which the membership responds if leadership is merged into a vague collage of differing personalities? In the absence of a clear personal image, the direction of human organization comes to be seen as an impersonal, controlling mechanism. A source of vitality has been lost in an effort to gain "efficiency."

And so it appears that human organization responds best where the focus of leadership is in a single person. With this premise, it is necessary to outline the ways in which that person most effectively fulfills his demanding role. For the sake of simplicity, let us concentrate on the elements of the role of a chief executive of a sizable organization. The comparable elements which appear in varying degrees of intensity in the functioning of subordinate line executives in a large organization can be assumed from the more comprehensive analysis of the role of the man at the top.

The unique role of the chief executive as a leader is to sustain, enhance, and project the personality of his organization through the impact of his own personality. If organizations are to be distinguished from machines and are to possess a human quality, the differentiation starts at the top. Subsidiary leaders can struggle to make a headless bureaucracy a friendly and comfortable place to work, but they cannot replace the influence of a corporate chief in demonstrating the purpose, traditions, standards, goals, and style of the whole organization.

The elevated position of the leader gives him a high degree of visibility. It is proper for the leader to assume that his acts, words, appearance, values, and style are a force for making a hierarchical grouping of human beings into an effective organization. This is not a cause for vanity, but rather for a deep sense of responsibility. In human organization a leader takes on a symbolic image whether he is a prime minister, a president, a general, or the manager of a factory. This image is a precious means of gaining response. It is no longer one's own to treat casually, but an important and sensitive resource of the organization one leads. Those who desire entire privacy should not aspire to leadership.

The leader's personality is projected into the organization through a multitude of daily contacts, discussions, decisions, and communications. But these channels need supplementation to counteract the loss of intensity which comes about as communication passes through many layers of the organization. Such reinforcement may come through the written—or preferably the spoken—word reaching a broader audience within the organization and outside. One age-old tradition in the strongest and most durable organizations calls for a personal appearance by the "head of state" on important occasions. Military reviews are a means of direct visual contact between a leader and his organization. The president of a university speaks at convocations. The modern corporation may have become technically efficient, but its leaders will misjudge the human nature of organization if they consider the projection of the leader's personality a sentimental diversion. The manner in which a leader in business, in a trade union, or a university today may make contact with his people varies, but anonymity and splendid isolation corrodes confidence, which is the basis of effective response. The president of a corporation may not be a Winston Churchill, but he is still in the business of leading people. To them he represents the personality of the corporation, its purposes, traditions, standards, goals, and style—whether he likes it or not.

It seems a paradox in the dynamics of human organization that the leader must, as an individual, be a visible symbol of the personality of the organization and, at the same time, develop all the arts of resolving the individual efforts of the members of the organization, *including his own*, into a coordinated team endeavor. As a symbol, he must be visible to gain response; as an operator, he must submerge his personal contribution in the combined efforts of the group. A leader without a sense of organization becomes a prima donna. The balance between symbol and co-worker is a delicate one that is not always easy to preserve. Although the traditions of organizations vary, the proliferation of administrative techniques has increased the difficulty of attaining that balance in larger organizations, because "channels" and decentralized operations keep people apart and the symbol is likely to fade.

The essence of organization is the subdivision of function, both in the areas to be covered and at the various levels of competency. The test of effectiveness is what will work, not any rigid *a priori* scheme. Unlike a machine, human organization must fit function to individual human capacity, position by position, and not assume that once a function is determined, a precisely fitted person can be inserted. A feeling for organization must include appreciation of order, but not in any static sense. Organization must be seen not as an abstract wall chart, but as a living reality, a structure of people with functions, capacities, interactions, and tensions. The ability to comprehend this structure in both objective and human terms, through mind and imagination, is the hallmark of an able leader.

The dangers of an inadequate sense of organization in a leader surface at the two extremes. If the value of organization as such is discounted, there is a tendency for the areas of responsibility to become fuzzy at the edges and for the interactions between individuals to develop more friction than reinforcement. Zones of assumed responsibility may overlap or may leave uncovered areas which no one seeks to fill. At the other extreme, excessive delimitation and rigidity in organizational assignments encourages bureaucracy and reduces the ready, informal reinforcement of one individual's efforts by another, which is the essence of good teamwork.

The selection of his immediate staff is the leader's most difficult challenge. Filling positions down the line may be done through standardized procedures, but the persons who report directly to the chief executive should have attributes which interact with his. This may involve both reinforcement and complementation. A leader's force and style should not be attenuated by an unsympathetic staff. At the same time, no leader can know all areas of concern equally well. A wise leader selects some aides whose temperament counterbalances his own, either in being more ready for change or more conservative, provided a full understanding of final responsibility is assured. Knowledgeable and sensitive people should evaluate the education, experience, reliability, and motivation of candidates for the leader's immediate staff, but the final selection should be made by the chief executive. It is he who must judge how well the candidate will work with him in the assignment he intends to give him. The emphasis must be upon the dynamics of interaction and not upon capabilities alone. If a leader is to gain response from his total organization, he needs the help of enthusiastic response at close hand.

Since the leader of a large organization must take final responsibility for many decisions, he is wise if he transmits a sense of total responsibility to his immediate staff. This encourages a subordinate to be concerned in the decisions and operations in areas outside his own direct responsibility. It also requires the subordinate to fill the vacuum, if any should develop, in assuring complete understanding and reasonable action in situations where coordination falters or delegation is unclear. The leader's immediate staff should epitomize the team play sought throughout organization. The assignment of direct responsibility for a specific area of operations should neither limit a subordinate's contribution to general policy nor give him an exclusive monopoly on wisdom in running his own show. It is the chief executive who sets the tone in blending his immediate staff into a mutually reinforcing policy team and not merely a group of specialists jealous of their authority. It is another reason why the leader's immediate staff needs far more than technical competency alone. The *human* nature involved in an executive team is a sensitive and critical manifestation of the human nature of the total organization.

An effective device for building a group of chief subordinates into a smoothly working team is to hold regularly scheduled staff meetings. Such meetings are not only a means of two-way communication between the leader and those reporting to him but also between those responsible for various functions within the organization. Staff meetings provide the occasion for airing ideas and gaining reactions to them while they are still in a tentative stage. It is the part of wisdom for a leader to encourage all who attend to offer their ideas, but he must create a climate in which ideas can be freely discussed and criticized without reflection upon the author. Even then, it is tactful for the leader to act as a moderator in encouraging others to participate in a freewheeling evaluation process rather than to be too ready to pass judgment before all have been heard. The wise handling of staff conferences has many by-products, not least of which is the opportunity for a leader to learn more fully the qualities of those he has chosen as his aides.

The free discussion of an issue in a climate of joint concern in no way releases the leader from full responsibility for making final decisions and implementing them. His shift from the role of moderator to that of decision maker, when all points of view have been expressed, must be clearly recognized by all concerned. The ability to encourage both free-wheeling discussion and unquestioned respect for the prerogatives and responsibilities of the chief executive, once decision is reached, is one of the fine arts of leadership. It involves the whole personality of the leader, not his knowledge alone. It also involves the personalities of the staff he has built around him and the way in which he has taught them his concept and style of leadership.

The classic example of the shift from discussion to decision concerns Abraham Lincoln when, in the midst of the Civil War, he made the mistake of polling his cabinet on a policy on which he had sought advice. Finding himself the only person voting aye, he sustained his role as leader by announcing, "The ayes have it." A leader should avoid counting heads in a policy discussion with his staff. It is the ideas that are important, not their authorship or their precise weighting on one side or another. A decision represents the judgment of the leader, not a majority vote of his staff. Regardless of outcome, the individual judgments of staff members must be considered a means to a single decision, not a recorded vote. An executive staff is not Congress; a recorded vote is uncalled for.

The frequency and urgency of staff consultation by a leader will, of course, vary greatly with the urgency or the seriousness of the decision to be made. Some decisions fall within general precedent. Others involve subtleties or unknowns in terms of both knowledge and values. The most difficult are those involving the uncertainties of human attitudes and response, whether inside or outside the organization. In the pressures of today's world, there is a tendency to foreshorten discussion, to overvalue tangible evidence, and to undervalue intuition. It is in discussion with his staff that the leader gains insights, hunches, and reactions about people, problems, and proposals and enriches his logical and intuitive processes. In addition, discussion releases the anxieties of those who must accept decision and enables them to execute policy with more understanding and enthusiasm. Even where the balance of advantage in decision is so close as to be uncertain, the fact that discussion has occurred gives moral weight to a leader's arbitrary choice of policy.

With a sense of organization, careful selection of his immediate subordinates, and wise decision-making procedures, a leader must still put organization into action. To do this, he must break down the elements of the policies and programs to be implemented and assign responsibility for their execution. This is the art of delegation. It is exercised at every stage of operation in hierarchical human organizations but, like many everyday acts, is seldom the subject of introspection. The aspects of delegation which involve a command-response balance and problems of communication will be discussed elsewhere. However, in dealing with the leader and his immediate staff, certain universal requirements of effective delegation assume critical importance because of the consequences of failure to meet them. For the leader, wise delegation is a demanding art.

While responsibility for many new policies or programs fall within the predetermined jurisdiction of particular subordinate officers, there is always the possibility that some other assignment might prove better. Organization and function are interacting, and both should be reviewed whenever new responsibilities are added. The leader's understanding of both his staff and the organization is essential if an assignment is to be matched to the man. Further essentials in delegation include clarity and precision in outlining the assignment given, including objectives, ways and means, authority and jurisdiction, time span allowed, and the coordination and reporting required. The best delegation involves a cycle of oral discussion, written direction, and oral discussion. What is clear in the mind of the leader must become clear to the delegate. Oral interchange enlarges the understanding of the written word, but the written word forces precise formulation. In delegation to a high-level subordinate, much greater freedom to use personal initiative, judgment, and responsibility is normal. The appropriate boundaries of freedom can often be agreed upon only by discussion of hypothetical possibilities or problems.

For the vigorous executive, proper delegation requires a careful equilibrium between the ever present tendency to expand one's area of decision-making power and the need to build a responsible, coordinated staff. If through excessive zeal for personal accomplishment he delegates too little, his effectiveness bogs down from overwork, subordinates become too dependent, and the morale and initiative of his organization decline. If, on the other hand, he delegates too much, he may lose control and encourage atomization of policy and competition for power. The appropriate degree of delegation of authority is not the same for diverse individuals, for diverse areas, or at different times. An invaluable backstop against errors in delegation is the art and practice of supervision, audit, and review.

Examples of the patterns of delegation may be helpful. Where the span of control is large, a leader may delegate greater responsibility to older, experienced subordinates and use his own time to develop younger executives to whom he delegates less. Delegation and review are the nub of executive development. Without some risk, initiative is cribbed in. Without sympathetic review and firm support, lessons are not learned and morale may suffer. It is often easier to tell a subordinate precisely what to do in a sticky situation than to let him work it out himself. Providing ready-made answers to problems is not teaching. It may boost the ego of the leader, but it does not contribute to the development of a responsible staff. The purpose of delegation is to multiply the effectiveness of the leader through the sharing of immediate and separable elements of responsibility.

It requires self-restraint on the part of the leader to avoid giving so much help to subordinates on delegated responsibilities that he hasn't sufficient time and energy for solving the tougher problems which cannot be delegated.

The shadowy line between excessive and insufficient supervision in respect to delegated responsibilities must be discovered case by case with each individual subordinate. The degree of initiative delegated can be made clear in particular situations when a subordinate asks for advice. At such times, the leader can gain a sense of the progress that has been made and of the major problems to be dealt with. An effective approach is to suggest possible considerations affecting possible decisions, not the decisions themselves. This might be termed the approach of "preventive medicine" in guiding subordinates. It often obviates later surgery.

But the apparatus of supervising delegated assignments involves far more than individual guidance. Both the subordinate executive and the total organization must demonstrate results in concrete terms. This involves the system of reports and audits normal to large organizations today. Such reports and their auditing are, without question, important in sustaining the effectiveness of operations in human organization. But like the score of a ball game, they deal with history and not the future, and with results rather than causes. From the point of view of sustaining effective organization, the value of reports lies more in their preparation than in their reading. Since formal reports usually omit information on *how* the results were attained and on the conditions surrounding the process, the leader is very likely to find such reports more a statistical record than a flow of vital, current information. The things the leader really has to know come up the line by less formal means through more general channels and from the people who are directly responsible. The leader is not obliged to await the visit of a subordinate but learns much by visiting him and his area of operations. Especially in respect to the tone of an organization—its enthusiasm, style, good order, and precision —much can be learned on the spot which neither statistical reports, correspondence, or even telephone calls will duplicate.

It is a danger in larger corporations today that the dynamics of leadership through person-to-person relations will become clouded by an excessive reliance upon mechanisms of control. Mechanisms of control emphasize precisely measurable data such as dollar outgos and incomes, tons, hours, square feet, and categories of personnel. The problem with such data is that it is always partial, abstract, and quantitative. And yet, because of its apparent precision, it is more impressive than qualitative judgments. If too much emphasis is placed by the leader on measurable results, the intangible qualitative attributes of effective administration may suffer. It is difficult to measure morale—or the growth of a person, or the loyalty of a labor force, or the dedication of officers in the face of adverse conditions—by statistics. Most human activities involve serving some constituency, but the bare bones of statistics fail to measure the attitudes of those served or the possibility of doing better.

Perhaps the simplest way to point up the difference between a leadership-centered and a control-centered management of human organization is to remind ourselves that dollars can be budgeted but human motivation can't. As a frame of reference in respect to funds available, budgets are essential. As a device for developing greater leadership, enthusiasm, dedication, reliability, cooperation, or for building the organization and improving its quality, budgets are a dull reflection of the machines used in their elaboration. There has, unfortunately, been more rapid progress in developing the machinery of accounting than in strengthening the capacity for leadership in human organization. It is high time that the more difficult challenge receives attention.

Among the arts of leadership which arise out of its essentially human orientation is that of sensing the optimum pace and timing for decisions or actions that affect people. Human nature abhors suddenness, especially when change in personal advantage, security, or convenience is involved. Further, persons who have ideas want to express them, and the process takes time. The leader himself will usually gain new insights if he allows a new policy to gestate for a while, so that his key aides have an opportunity to offer their reactions and suggestions. The advance notice that a problem is under consideration warns all parties that change is possible or imminent without final commitment.

A special need for anticipation exists where a chief executive must gain confirmation and support of his decisions from a board of directors or trustees. As persons of authority and concern, the members of such boards are even more disturbed by suddenness than subordinates, since their views are supposed to carry weight. A rule in dealing with boards is to present an issue during at least three meetings: in the first, to describe the problem and the considerations in dealing with it; in the second, to outline tentative and preliminary conclusions; and in the third, to recommend specific action. This rule of three requires not only anticipation but also adequate opportunity for clear exposition and free discussion. A brief mention of a new idea does not give board members enough to chew on. The chances are good that the more fully a chief executive explains an important problem to his board, the more likely it is that the board will rely upon his judgment in solving it. The return on the investment of early communication and discussion is not only better and more timely advice while alternatives are still open, but also more knowing support when final decision is reached. Confidence in human relations grows out of mutual understanding, whereas a vacuum of ignorance leaves too much room for doubt.

In no aspect of leadership is anticipation more necessary than when immediate subordinates hold conflicting positions on issues of considerable significance. That differences in temperament, approaches, and intuitive assumptions exist within an executive group is not only normal but wholesome. Without countervailing tensions, a human organization tends to lose tone and vitality. The task of the leader is to capitalize on the differences among his staff as a means of assuring a comprehensive review of alternatives against the broad frame of reference of overall company policy. This takes time and free discussion, and demands the direct and insightful guidance of the leader. The emphasis must be upon the ideas and evidence advanced, with a conscious goal of seeking a consensus for the good of the organization. It is most important to prevent crystallization of personal positions through either pride or self-interest. An astute and respected leader can usually find a way to resolve issues which lifts the level of a merged consensus above that of an arbitrary verdict for one side or another.

Contrary to the usual assumption, the most difficult conflicts to resolve are not those for which complex but *tangible* pro and con evidence can be marshaled, but rather those in which intangible factors or intuitive judgments are involved. Objective, quantifiable evidence can be tested and weighed by specialists until a reasonable finding is attained. Where differences arise concerning such matters as fair dealing with people either inside or outside the organization, the timing and pace of change, the traditions and goals of the organization, or the probabilities of the distant future, judgments are so subtle and subjective that the leader must be ready to relieve his staff of the responsibility to reach consensus. In such judgments, the personality of the leader is reflected in the personality of the organization. Yet, even in these difficult and lonely decisions, anticipation and discussion afford the leader the opportunity to explain and test his conclusions while they are still tentative, even though he knows that the final decision must be his own.

To handle the accumulation of these broad, less tangible issues, the leader of a large organization today must develop the power of conceptualization. This is an end product of a personal system of values, judgments, and goals which has been thought through and tested both rationally and intuitively against experience over many years. Such a conceptual system enables the leader to ask the right questions when all sorts of evidence has been marshaled by both those who want to promote a given policy and those who oppose it. It is here that the subtle and wide-ranging powers of the human mind far exceed the competence of a computer. In the well-trained mind, a host of variables from the concrete to the abstract, the certain to the uncertain, the immediate to the distant in time or effect or concern to one's organization and one's community can be weighed, integrated, and tested against an evolving system of basic values, judgments, and intuitive assumptions. The ability to develop and clearly conceptualize such personal norms and to apply them with courage and sensitivity in deciding complex issues has become the essential role of the leader in large organizations today.

IV

Communication

IT HAS BEEN SAID that communication is organization in action. In human organization, leadership depends upon the communication of an understanding of mission, means, and method to effect response, both rational and emotional, in the human beings who form the organization. Since both the initiation and response in this process of communication are man-centered, the *human* nature of this aspect of organization is clear. The complex of technical devices which have come to facilitate the process of communication in larger organizations tends to divert attention from the essential truth that effective communication is more a matter of minds than of machines.

As human organizations have grown in size from those in which the leader can communicate face to face and frequently with each member of his team to those which involve many layers of subordinates and distances in space and time, the problems of communication have multiplied almost at a geometric rate. The reasons for this lie far more in the *human* aspects of the process than in the technical means used. It is necessary, therefore, to analyze these human aspects of communication to determine how they can—and cannot—promote effective leadership and sensitive response in the large organizations of today.

All communication beyond the simplest form of face-to-face interaction involves symbols. Even the gesture that indicates good-bye is a symbol, and, what's more, it varies from culture to culture. The symbols for abstract numbers are probably the most standardized, especially for quantities up to ten, but these also vary from language to language. Even expressions for large numbers vary throughout the world. The Japanese, for example, do not think in terms of millions in the way natural to us.

It is when symbols must be used in the communication of ideas, values, qualities, or judgments that communication tends to go to sea, because words themselves are only symbols. Ordering a thousand bricks of precise dimensions to build a wall is a simple act of communication. But what of their color, content, and durability? In most acts of communication, many imprecise factors are inherent even though they may not be recognized as such.

The nub of the matter is that in any process of communication *two* translations occur. The sender must translate the conceptualization in his mind into a symbol. The receiver must translate that symbol into a conceptualization in his mind. The sender assumes all too readily that it will merge with his own. To give a very simple illustration, one can say that this is a "good" apple. The speaker's conceptualization of an approved apple in terms of taste, smell, color, and firmness of texture is translated in his mind into the symbol "good." The recipient of the message must then translate the symbol "good" into *his* conceptualization of the proper taste, smell, texture, and color of an approved apple. This two-way translation is a matter of much more than academic interest to those who are concerned with effective organization. It has profound, far-reaching effects on even day-to-day operations.

Examples of word symbols used in the communication of company policy are numberless. An executive tells his subordinates that employees must be given "fair" treatment. The meaning of the word "fair" in the mind of the executive has taken its shape from a complex of values, experience, and both conscious and unconscious assumptions which are unique to him. Likewise, the many subordinates down the line introduce their individually unique values, experience, and conscious or unconscious assumptions into their translation of the symbol. The range of interpretation may wreck the morale of an organization if it is not recognized that this seemingly simple message involves a whole system of human elements and responses in an ongoing organization. Many strikes have occurred because the meaning of the symbol "fair" was mistranslated.

Let us pursue this word as an example. When a leader uses the symbol "fair" it is charged with his personality, both as he sees himself and as others see him. The symbol may be interpreted as merely what he wants others to assume rather than what is truly an outward expression of his structured and consistent system of values. If his values are to be correctly interpreted, he must be known to the person who receives his message. Where values are involved, the sender of the message is *a part of the message*. Because of this, the symbol has very little meaning until the user is known, at least by reputation, to the person who receives the message.

The interpretation of a symbol charged with value content is not a distinct and separate event, but a part of a continuing flow of communication, overt and implied, in words, acts, and assumptions. The word "fair" will be far more definite to a group of subordinates who have worked together under an executive for many years than to a newly organized group. The defining of the symbol is a process which may require testing and retesting over a long period of time against actual events. Definition, as the word implies, is the marking out of the boundaries of what is included in a symbol. Legal opinions are full of such definitions. To take an illustration from constitutional law, the interpretation of the word symbol "reasonable" has filled volumes.

One very great difficulty in dealing with value judgments as they are expressed in words has to do with their ingrained, deep-set nature. The notion of what is fair starts developing in early childhood. It is a part of one's cultural development, in the family, the school, the gang, and the community. To test this, ask yourself when is it fair to report the misbehavior of another person to someone in authority, whether the person is a friend, a classmate, a neighbor, or a total stranger. Word symbols whose meaning derives from diverse politico-cultural backgrounds are a source of much misunderstanding in all forms of human organization. They include "freedom," "loyalty," "democracy," "human rights," "law and order," "justice," "fair-dealing," "sportsmanship," "self-respect," "good manners," "responsibility," "patriotism," and "national interest."

It might be argued that word meanings are more precise where communications deal with content which is specific and practical. This might be true if such content could be neatly separated from value judgments. An enthusiastic executive proposes a change in a manufacturing process or in a sales approach. He may do a first-rate job of explaining the proposal clearly and presenting its advantages persuasively, but any change may affect the vested interests, convenience, or sense of past accomplishment of the persons involved. The result is that an otherwise rational process of exposition arouses reactions of caution, doubt, or resistance quite apart from the logical proof of advantage to the organization. It is difficult for the recipient of communication to turn off his emotions and concentrate on the rational analysis of meaning, even though the language is lucid, objective, and otherwise persuasive.

It is clear that even communication of content which appears divorced from values or emotions is seldom free of subjective overtones that reflect the feelings of both the sender and the receiver. This is particularly true in the communications within a closed organization where there is a hierarchical relationship between them. The exception might be the routine transmission of statistical or technical data in which neither party is called upon to interpret or act. The human aspect of communications is introduced where *response* is involved.

Where communication involves the exposition of complex data, even if all parties involved are rational, objective, and unconcerned with philosophical overtones, there remains the problem of the transfer of the conceptualization of the sender to the conceptualization of the receiver. The human mind is a marvelous thing, but it has no magical power to comprehend something entirely outside its previous experience or knowledge. Training and education, from infancy to adulthood, is largely a matter of making symbols meaningful as people are exposed to increasingly complex material. A baby learns the symbol for a horse by having mother point to a horse and explicitly identifying it with the spoken word. It is interesting to note that the word symbol for horse among many American Indian tribes is "big dog." Never having seen a horse until the Spaniards introduced the animal, the Indians simply had no word for it. On the other hand, the Eskimos have developed generation by generation many distinct word symbols for what most people in warmer climates are content to call snow.

The development of a vast system of meaningful word symbols by the human mind is a marvelous process, but even more awesome is the growth of comprehension of complex concepts symbolized by an intellectual shorthand covering the entire spectrum of human learning and activity. A random collection of such symbols might include "atom," "plasma," "genes," "evolution," "quantum," "solid-state," "catalysis," "jet propulsion," "balance of payments," "business cycle," "oligopoly," "jurisprudence," "constitution," "renaissance," "poetry," "style," "linguistics," "dialectics," and "salvation." Yet all these expressions are the accepted symbols of communication among those who have come to understand the concepts they stand for. Those concerned with the process of communication in organization should be interested in learning how such understanding develops.

A fundamental principle in developing the understanding of the symbols of communication is that the human mind moves from the known to the unknown. The Eskimo from childhood "knew" his snow in all its conditions. The American Indian needed to move mentally from an ordinary dog to a "big dog" to produce a generally comprehensible symbol for a horse. The individual attempting to comprehend a concept represented by a symbol new to him associates that symbol with the nearest known concepts based on his experience or observation. That is a powerful aid to understanding, but it is also the source of great danger if not safeguarded by a corrective process. The corrective process encompasses the whole universe of interactive education, informal and formal, between those who comprehend a symbol clearly and those who don't. It is an essential element in all education. Without the accumulation of meaningful symbols, corrected by both informal and formal education, life as we know it in modern times would be impossible, because our means of communicating anything more than the simple needs for survival would not exist.

An example of the hazards inherent to the process of moving from the known to the unknown in approaching a new and complex concept is the great difference which exists throughout the world in the conceptual response to the symbol-word "democracy." A Russian cannot understand why Americans hold the word in reverence since to the Russian it has overtones of an unwieldy and massive town meeting unguided by intelligent and far-seeing leadership. "Democracy" to an African may mean the elimination of oppression and little more. To a villager in Southeast Asia, it may mean continued oppression under a government supported from abroad.

To assure that the symbols used in the vital process of communication in the leadership of an organization come through clearly and accurately requires a sustained system of interaction between the sender and the receiver of the messages employing those symbols. The more complex the concepts symbolized, the more rigorous must be that interaction. The process is one of exposition and questioning, clarification and discussion, illustration and counterillustration, and the sharpening of the differentiation from other concepts. This is, again, an educational process. It is also communication at its best, especially where complex ideas, plans, or policies involve key terms or phrases.

A rewarding exercise for anyone interested in the art of communicating ideas is to study the way in which the great leaders of the world have made sure that the word symbols in their messages took on clarity and force in the mind of the receiver. The greatest leader of all time sought to convey the idea that "Thou shalt love thy neighbor as thyself." When asked to clarify the meaning of "neighbor," he told the parable of the Good Samaritan. Every element of the story of the Jericho road was clearly understandable to his disciples. The particular road had a bad reputation; travelers, robbers, inns, and innkeepers were well known to everyone. A vague and debatable symbol became sharply defined and vital in the demanding ethical principle Christ sought to convey.

In the communication of ideas, parables and analogies can be anything from a single word to a whole book, depending upon the intellectual resources or the emotional sensitivity of the people who are party to the communication. Names—real or fictitious—like Job, Judas, Caesar, Romeo, Machiavelli, Caspar Milquetoast, and Scrooge create associations which conceptualize human behavior. *Uncle Tom's Cabin* and *The Christmas Carol* were parables. Fables have given us dog in the manger, sly fox, and sour grapes. There are hundreds of sayings in every language which express folk wisdom in parables or analogies such as "Chickens come home to roost," "Pour out the baby with the bath," "Burn the candle at both ends," and "Lock the barn door after the horse is stolen." The sender of a message has endless resources to call upon to reinforce or interpret the more conventional symbols used in communication.

The art of stimulating appropriate associations in the mind of the receiver is to use the most relevant and dramatic parable or analogy which reinforces meaning without diverting attention from the main thrust of the message. An illustrative allusion must fall within the general principle that one uses the known to make clear what has so far been vaguely comprehended, confusing, or unknown. The danger lies in using analogies which do not closely parallel the meaning to be communicated, merely because they are colorful. It is almost as bad to use analogies and trite expressions that have lost their value through excessive or inaccurate use. Cliché-ridden speech has a deadly effect.

This excursion into the complexities of human communication has seemed necessary because of the assumption of Americans, especially, that communication can be taken for granted as long as everyone concerned speaks English. The files of most executives are filled with dull, prolix policy statements, directives, memoranda, and letters which are full of word symbols representing concepts which are loosely defined in the mind of the author and still more loosely defined in the minds of the recipients. Telephone conversations may give some opportunity for clarification, and face-to-face discussion may eliminate some uncertainties. But such discussions are usually brief, and a subordinate is usually too inhibited to indicate uncertainty. The worst that can happen as the result of hurried direct communication is that two people may each be certain of the other's meaning when they have not in fact understood it at all.

Several conclusions can be drawn from this analysis. First, if communication is to be an activating force in organization, the leader must not only clearly understand the vast range of concepts with which he deals; he must also be educated in the precise and demanding art of translating these concepts into words, sentences, and paragraphs that accurately convey his meaning to his readers or listeners. In addition, his symbols and total exposition must serve to activate the response he is seeking. Response is the nub of the problem, and response is a very human thing. Confusion between the mechanical vehicles of communication and an essentially human process can lead to the failure of organization itself.

A second conclusion is that communication in a closed organization should be an interactive process, to the fullest extent possible, where anything other than the most concrete or measurable subject matter is concerned. A written message is not exact if the word symbols it uses do not translate into identical concepts at both ends of the process. Therefore, the bracketing-in of meaning through oral, face-to-face discussion is essential. The written message is thus reinforced and stands as a record of a mutually confirmed understanding.

A third conclusion is that communication in a closed organization is seldom a single act but is, rather, an evolving, reinforcing system encompassing far more than any discrete message. In the course of this evolution, how senders conceptualize symbols becomes known to receivers and vice versa. Past messages, as well as past actions related to them, become relevant to the interpretation of new messages. Past responses affect the content of new efforts to gain response. That is why seasoned organizations, like seasoned basketball teams, do better than newly formed organizations, even with better members.

A fourth conclusion, which correlates with our earlier discussion of the attributes of the leader in human organization, is this: in the most important area of communication in an ongoing organization—that concerned with values, purposes, standards, and motivation—the personality of the sender is part of the message. It was Nelson and not an anonymous lieutenant who sent the message at Trafalger, "England expects every man to do his duty." If, like some present-day politicians, Nelson had permitted a credibility gap to develop, the response to the symbols "England," "every man," and "duty" would have been far different.

But how can the art of exposition, interaction, systematic flow, and personal character be combined to enhance communication in the large, many-tiered organizational structures of today? The best suggestion produced by years of observation is to build a system of interlocking links in the chain of communication down through and up through the total organization. By interlocking links is meant an arrangement whereby any important message, from any focus of leadership, is transmitted, not by the written word alone, but is reinforced by interactive discussion between one level (the leader) and the next lower level. The process continues downward from level to level. Such interactive discussion, level to level, trains in the art of exposition and permits the clarification of meaning at many checkpoints. By repetition, it builds up a systematic flow of two-way communication in which receiver becomes sender. It makes each sender a part of the message. The written word remains important as a point of common reference throughout the organization, but the words take on more nearly common meaning to people distant from the original source.

The staff conference in many organizations is intended to provide an interlocking system of communications. The usual shortcomings, however, are their infrequency, their limitation to senior levels, and their often perfunctory character. Executives at all levels feel that they are too busy to take the time for meetings and persuade themselves that a directive or memo will do. If the directive is not understood, a telephone conversation with a questioner or two becomes the inadequate substitute for group discussion which would clarify the mind of the author as well as the understanding of the whole group of recipients.

It is a mistake to assume that group discussion is the privilege of the higher command, that less-senior personnel, even though they may be leaders of groups of sub-leaders, should not be included in a chain of interlocking discussion. How can such discussion assure effective communication and response without their participation? It has been known for years that foremen are an important key to effective operations and have much influence upon communication to the rank and file.

The perfunctory character of many staff conferences is a reflection on the qualifications and understanding of the leader. A leader who does not understand the complexities of effective interactive communication, or who assumes that leadership means command rather than the development of response, is unlikely to create the climate necessary for an effective staff conference. A good leader has, instinctively, the approach of a good teacher. He is concerned about developing understanding and is not satisfied with passive acceptance of directions which may or may not approximate his intent. Communication by the process of discussion remains an art. It is not easily acquired by those who are unsure of their status or their capacity to handle the issues and material covered. Even where status and ability are unquestioned, a leader must learn the art of stimulating meaningful, relevant, and effective interactive discussion that is correlative to the importance of the subject at hand.

Communication *is* organization in action. The human nature of communication within organization reinforces the human character of the whole. With the increasing size and complexity of governmental units, corporations, and other institutions today, great strain has been put upon the system of communication needed to keep any organization an integrated and dynamic social organism. No matter how many electronic devices are developed as the passive vehicles of transmission, the real test of cohesion and continued growth will be the ability of human beings to understand clearly the meaning of the messages they receive so that they can act with intelligence and zeal.

V

Tradition

TRADITION IS the time dimension in human organization. It has far more influence upon the effectiveness and survival of human organizations than is commonly realized. Its essential thrust is intangible, working through men's minds. It may be symbolized in many outward forms, but essentially it is an evolving, pervasive system of assumptions, habits of mind, customary behavior, and attitudes which stamps an organization with a distinct personality by predisposing its members to think and act in a way generally favorable to the survival of the organization.

The importance of tradition in human organization can be sensed by examining what keeps an organization going when leadership, membership, or conditions change, even drastically. A machine wears out and falls apart. A tree or a man grows old and dies. But something within a coordinated combination of changing individuals may, under favorable conditions, insure the continuance of that combination as a corporate personality for centuries. Whether it is Oxford University or the Roman Catholic Church, other accomplishments notwithstanding, an essential factor is tradition. But tradition is also an essential source of survival in any organization that outlives the throes of its creation. An able leader may so impose his personality on an organization that for a time he is the temporary embodiment of that organization's tradition. But when he passes or conditions change, tradition must pervade the organization itself or it too will disappear.

There is a tendency, especially in America, to confine the term "tradition" to quaint and outmoded ceremonies, patriotic observances, or manifestations of institutional nostalgia. But there is no better word to encompass that momentum in human behavior and attitudes which insures that a thousand diverse individuals will perform their assigned duties in a complex of coordinated operations with minimal direction day after day. Not only performance per se but the quality of performance and the way in which people work together involve something drawn from the past which reaches into the future. It is not merely response to ever present authority. It is a predisposition developed in each person from the time he became a part of the ongoing organization.

Extreme examples of tradition as a continuing force in organization are found in the military. A Marine Corps sergeant seeks to instill a traditional response in the new recruit. The traditions of the Royal Navy pervade daily life aboard British ships. But less obvious to a passenger aboard a train or plane are the traditions that are buried in the routines performed by dispatchers, towermen, engineers, pilots, navigators, and others in moving trains and planes over great distances. Even when emergencies occur, predetermined procedures reinforce discretionary judgments in getting the job done. In less colorful endeavors, the degree to which tradition, or its manifestation in routine, pervades the operations of a factory, bank, office, or school is far greater than is realized until this persistent momentum in human organization is lost for a time by strikes, fires, floods, or other misfortunes.

Tradition, in its fullest sense, takes its place along with leadership and communication as one of the three primary elements in effective human organization. In large degree, it is the projection of past leadership as it has permeated human organization through interactive response. Just as such interactive response assures cohesion and effectiveness in organization in a single time frame, so tradition assures cohesion and effectiveness—again through communication—over an extended period of time. The three elements are not only primary but closely interactive. Each, fully understood and properly developed, can go far in assuring the effective combination of human beings in a joint enterprise.

But the fundamental importance of tradition in

human organization does not assure its beneficial effect if it is not continuously influenced by the interaction of leadership and communication. There can be
bad traditions, obsolete traditions, wasteful traditions,
and traditions which are obstacles to progress. The
traditions of criminal gangs, corrupt political rings, or
old-time pirate crews have been powerful factors in
controlling such organizations in their pursuit of gain.
Women have long suffered under the traditions of
enterprises or professions dominated by men. Craft
unions, in the name of tradition, have often sought to
require employers to use more men on a job than
changed conditions warranted. Traditions have sometimes held back progress by their controlling influence
upon the minds of all levels of management as well as
of the rank and file.

A subtle but pervasive influence of tradition on
human organization has been the persistent assumption
that length of service in an organization should auto-
matically justify preferment. This tradition, if uncon-
trolled, leads not only to the loss in efficiency otherwise gained by wiser methods of determining preferment but also to the entrenchment of tradition itself,
since those of longer service are more likely to per-
petuate the past.

The sad history of most American railroads ex-
emplifies what an overdose of tradition supported by
seniority and lacking the antidote of farseeing leadership can do to great corporations. In earlier years,
each major railroad was saturated with corporate

pride from top to bottom. To be a railroad man, whether president or locomotive engineer, set one apart. The president had his private car, and the engineer blew the whistle. The tradition of hierarchical prestige in operations that were heavily loaded with routine created a climate conducive to seniority, elaborate rules and jurisprudence, smugness at the top, and opposition to change throughout. The coming of the automobile and the airplane seemed no cause for concern. Despite last-minute efforts to recoup, tradition and the effects of seniority so permeated the railroads as human organizations that new leadership could do little to save them.

It is unfair to limit to any particular kind of enterprise the examples of organizations in which tradition has curtailed the initiative of leadership. Most organizations go through cycles in balancing the two elements. Churches, legislative bodies, military establishments, public utilities, banks, steel corporations, and medical associations will indicate the range of examples of all stages of resistance to change and recovery of vigor. The trouble is not that traditions exist, but that they get out of hand. It is interesting to note that corrective measures are seldom initiated at the bottom. Fundamentally, only revitalized leadership can save the organization from hardening of the arteries and death.

That people are the essential ingredient in tradition as a factor in the survival of organizations is evidenced in the history of American railroads. The

multiplication of rules and a complex system of jurisprudence in their interpretation could not provide a
safeguard against slow decay in institutional cohesion
and vitality. Rather, rules and their adjudication
shifted emphasis toward external controls upon the
actions of individuals and away from the internal
assumptions of each individual that he should perform
effectively his part of a total mission. The rights of
individuals in our society are supported by great traditions, but in the pursuance of a common purpose in a
mutually interdependent organization, it is the tradition of individual obligation and responsibility to that
purpose which is central. A constant concern about
rights and rules does not make for effective team play
in either football or industry.

If the activating force in tradition is the combined
assumptions, habits of mind, customary behavior, and
attitudes of the individuals who make up an organization, the desired effect is *constructive response*. In any
but the crudest forms of physical endeavor, the quality
of response of the individual is far more influenced by
his personal assumptions and attitudes than by fear
of authority. The challenge of leadership is how to
utilize the force of tradition so that it enhances constructive response without permitting tradition to become embodied in rigid forms or practices which reduce effectiveness or retard progress. The effort
should be to strengthen the sense of responsibility
within the individual and to guard against too much
dependence upon the external justification of rules

and precedents. Harmful and wasteful traditions need to be pruned out by specific discouragement, but constructive traditions can only develop over time through the persistent convictions of respected leaders or associates, not through preachments.

An interesting example of the wise nurturing of tradition is the safety movement in American industry. In an earlier time, it was thought to be manly and courageous for a workman in a dangerous occupation to be unconcerned about risk even when it might be avoided. Some progress was made by requiring safer working conditions and developing a system of rules. But only when the traditional attitude of the individual workman was changed from one of unthinking tolerance of risk to a high regard for safety was satisfactory progress made. Safe operations became a way of life based upon individual assumptions reinforced by the traditions of the organization. The arts employed in changing traditional assumptions in the safety movement were many. Success came only when response based on internal assumptions rather than external control became the central focus of the movement.

There are many other examples of how traditional ways of life in American industry have been changed for the better by focusing on individual and group assumptions. One category concerns good housekeeping, cleanliness, pleasant work environment, sanitation, and orderliness. As men had more attractive homes, they assumed that they should have more attractive work places. Progressive employers have learned the truth of the old saying that men form structures and structures form men. The traditions of the British House of Commons or an ancient university are indeed reinforced—if only to a limited extent—by their physical structures. Sloppy work and sloppy thinking are less likely to occur where a traditional assumption of orderliness is symbolized in one's physical environment.

But the most important traditions in the survival and progress of organizations are those which involve values and goals. It is in these intangibles that the influence of leadership, past and present, is paramount. Here is where the statement that tradition is the projection of past leadership is clearly justified. Since values and goals become expressed by the acts of the leader far more clearly than by his words, the acts of leadership in the past are the substance of ongoing tradition for the future. It is the assumptions that underlie these acts that come through loud and clear to the members of an organization. The assumptions of the leader, made manifest in a continuing series of actions, become the assumptions of the follower. There is no shortcut through high-sounding preachments unsupported by actions, because preachments carry no conviction.

It has been said that a tradition of fair treatment for employees takes at least ten years to establish throughout a large corporation, but that it can be undermined in ten minutes by the unwise handling of a single critical situation. This may be an exaggeration, but experience suggests that it is nearer truth than fiction. The unfortunate acts of subordinates may be isolated from the mainstream of corporate assumptions if corrected in time. It is when the higher echelons of management depart from a long-accepted policy of fair dealing that real trouble ensues. This is why carefully developed grievance procedures are not only a protection for individual employees but also for those managements which seek to preserve a valuable tradition.

Other traditions which come to pervade a well-led organization over time are those influencing assumptions of dedication, responsibility, excellence, service, integrity, and loyalty. In a church or university these traditions are deep-seated and consciously respected. It is sometimes difficult in old institutions like these to determine just how these traditions have been transmitted from generation to generation with such a high degree of effectiveness. It is clear that they are far more the consequence of a thousand personal interactions than eloquent formal preachments.

But the same elements of tradition pervade in varying degrees every effective organization whether a regiment, a corporation, a bank, a hospital, an airline, or a department store. It is not popular to use highflown language invoking company spirit in the daily communications between a supervisor and his subordinates, so that the traditions of an organization seem to be highlighted more when they are broken than when they are observed. Such traditions are norms, and not all live up to them. But it is in the nature of ongoing human organizations for the members thereof to develop assumptions compatible with the norms of their leaders. Here again we see the critical role the leader plays in human organization.

It would be wonderful, indeed, if someone could invent a shortcut to the development of tradition. It reminds one of the story of the wealthy American tourist being shown around Oxford by the vice chancellor. At the end of their walk, the visitor asked his host, "What does it take to develop a great university like this?" The vice chancellor replied, "Five hundred years." It would have been more accurate to answer, "Five hundred inspired leaders spread over the centuries dedicated to scholarship and teaching." But the story illustrates the truth that tradition in organization is an intangible by-product that cannot be bought and sold but must grow out of the personality of men transmitted to the personality of the organizations they lead. There is no shortcut in this subtle operation.

It remains true that traditions are primarily sustained by men and not external forms, no matter how elaborate. Rituals and rules may embody tradition, but they are empty forms unless they are meaningful to those who practice them. The conduit of tradition is the overlapping succession of members of an organization who transmit the assumptions of the past and not merely the attitudes of the present. This introduces the question, How fast and to what extent can change occur in the human constituents of an organization without adversely affecting its beneficial traditions?

Individual human beings abhor suddenness, and organized groups of human beings abhor it greatly. There must always be change, and change must alter the detailed ways in which tradition is implemented, but it is of critical importance that change not proceed so fast or so far that *basic* traditions are endangered. The change that has most influence on basic traditions is that of men, not methods. A sudden displacement of a considerable segment of a leadership hierarchy can be devastating. A high turnover of rank and file can impair the process of transmitting tradition by day-to-day interactions and example.

It is the wise leader who balances a rate of change to gain technical efficiency with the rate of change that assures the continuity of valuable traditions. New managers may be more intelligent, more up to date, and more vigorous than those they replace, but they *are* new and unknown to their subordinates in respect to the assumptions which count in the sustaining of tradition. If new employees overbalance the old, traditions which have developed over the years and have been passed from worker to worker may be washed away in the flood of new and diverse assumptions.

Each type of organization tends to develop its own measures of how rapidly change can come without impairing valuable tradition. The established churches of the world, with essential traditions to preserve, have favored a long process for developing leadership and slow change in personnel. Popes and patriarchs, by their titles, are fatherly persons. An old residential university, which also embodies vital traditions, gives tenure to its faculty and admits but a fourth of its normal student body each year. Its president and deans are likely to be professors as well. Increasingly, American corporations have recognized the value of tempering change in the building of personnel in order to sustain valuable traditions. As a result, executives are more likely to be developed within the corporation and many programs will be designed to reduce employee turnover. Along with other advantages, the control of change in personnel is aimed at preserving the best in the traditions of the organization without a loss in the dynamism which leadership must also instill.

The American railroads were not wrong in respecting the value of tradition in building and sustaining human organization. They were wrong in not balancing tradition with the leadership needed to focus the efforts of organizations, strengthened by tradition, upon new goals and the methods required to attain them. In this lies a lesson for every student and practitioner in the field of human organization.

VI

Incentive

How DOES THE LEADER of an organization motivate its members to attain their common purpose? The question may be simple, but the answer to it involves insights drawn from the whole range of the social sciences as well as from practical experience. Again the key to the answer lies in the understanding individual response, in this case *incentive*. Incentive is as complex a phenomenon as human nature itself. How does a leader create and use an elaborate system for channeling the diverse and multiple incentives of the members of his organization into a joint effort, which hopefully will be more effective than the sum of the separate efforts of the members acting individually?

To use an illustration from primitive times, our caveman ancestors in ice-age Europe faced the problem of killing a mammoth to feed themselves and their families. Since the mammoth was too big to handle by individual effort, a leader was chosen to direct a joint attack. It was the leader's job to channel the motivation of hunger in each of his followers into a coordinated exercise of zeal and skill which set fear aside and brought the great beast down. The organization might have been simple and temporary, but the role of incentive to make it operative was just the same as that in General Motors today to build a million automobiles. The only difference is that in our civilized times, individual incentive involves far more subtle influences than hunger overcoming fear.

For the student of organization, the most interesting aspects of incentive are those reinforced by organization. But one has to start with the individual, the essential particle out of which organizations are developed. The caveman had a feeling in his stomach that craved satisfaction, which required vigorous effort. But he also had a fear of mammoths that might have told him to run. The zeal he demonstrated in the attack may have been enhanced by pride in self, a want of recognition, the excitement of combat, the desire for a sense of accomplishment, and even a hatred of mammoths. The essential point is that individual incentive may arise from a whole bundle of responses to a situation, in rapidly changing combination and intensity. He who deals with individual incentives has left the neat and tidy area where factors can be abstracted, measured, and compared like a chemist analyzing a compound.

It is interesting to speculate how individual incentives shift as conditions change and as the person gains sophistication. As Robinson Crusoe gained assurance that he would not starve or die of thirst, he sought a more comfortable way of life and the higher satisfactions of accomplishment. His instinctive drives may have given way to aesthetic and moral sentiments, but there remained the basic urge to work in order to avoid loss of security. As a higher animal, he was a captive of the urges for survival. Yet even with no one else present to admire his results, he still possessed the human attribute of self-evaluation. This interplay of the instinctive, emotional, and rational factors working on the individual personality is the substance of human motivation and incentive.

When an individual becomes part of an organization, he finds himself surrounded by forces which influence the operation of his individual system of incentives. One way to try to understand how this influence is exercised is to analyze incentives one at a time and determine how the leader can best use channels of organization to make them work to advance the purposes he seeks.

One of the oldest drives to joint action is fear of adversity, imminent or distant. The uses of fear in motivating the members of a group range from that of the whip in building the pyramids to the fear of reprimand or discharge in a modern factory. Both are crude stimuli, even if apparently effective, because their influence upon incentive is through the emotions rather than through self-initiated, rational determination. If the members of an organization are led to work by fear alone, then the pressure of fear must be sustained. There develops a subtle shift from the incentive to work to the incentive to avoid discipline. The ingenuity of the human mind, once concentrated upon an effort to avoid discipline, is extraordinary, especially in group activity. The art of the leader is to turn such ingenuity to constructive ends and to reserve the exercise of the crude instrument of fear for use in extreme cases of irresponsibility where the group as a whole will recognize it as an exception to their normal expectations.

But fear as a source of incentive can operate in more subtle ways than through the displeasure of an overseer. In a competitive world, organizations must compete for success or survival as well as individuals. The fear of layoff of a whole group or of marginal members thereof because of lack of work is, indeed, a stimulus to effort if it can be seen that effort will produce favorable results. The danger is that if the demand for their services appears to be fixed regardless of their efficiency, the workers may seek to spread that demand over as long a period as possible. It is, therefore, questionable how far a leader can exploit the fear of layoff as an incentive to effort. Experience indicates that the positive approach of communicating the possibilities of expanding demand through improved product or service is far more effective.

A special case of the interplay between fear of layoff and incentive has appeared time and again where labor-saving machinery or other technological changes affecting employment have been introduced. Studies have shown that anticipation and planning for all possible arrangements for alternative employment are necessary to avoid an adverse effect on incentive where there is uncertainty about continued employment. To avoid the adverse effects of insecurity, employers have established programs for dismissal compensation to buy out the expectancies of those for whom changed conditions eliminate the demand for their services. The effort is to attenuate the uncertainty of all by compensating the certain loss of some.

Both organizations and communities suffer from the by-products of fear and uncertainty. If concern for the present is excessive, constructive concern for the future is sacrificed. And if the sense of risk is high, the discounting of the future may become exaggerated. The temptation is to enjoy the present and let the future take care of itself. This attitude affects the behavior of soldiers in war as well as those living on the brink of need at any time. Its manifestations are gambling, recklessness, laziness, and intemperance. But it also appears in absenteeism, turnover, and slack work. It explains the difficulty of creating effective incentives for marginal groups who have not had the satisfaction of steady, gainful employment.

If fear and uncertainty are inefficient instruments for developing incentive in human organization, is the reverse, the opportunity for security, an effective means? It appears to be so if set about by appropriate arrangements under which security is assured. Security at a minimal level of life has produced some of the most backward peoples on earth. It is when incentive arises out of seeking a *higher level* of security that the latter becomes a powerful agent. It has been a tremendous force in the progress of America. It has been the means of expanding our frontiers and of building great enterprises. The problem is how to make a higher level of security a precise and proportionate reward for those who have earned it through incentive.

In the practical terms of business, the arrangements for assuring a *higher level* of security as a reward for incentive include the whole apparatus of effective evaluation of effort, skill, judgment, and cooperation which, joined together, produce the teamwork that is essential to success in modern enterprises. Executive and staff ratings, wage and salary administration, promotion, and fringe benefits are all a part of the system. The purpose of all these programs is the judicious rewarding of past incentive and the encouragement of continued incentive. The substance of the reward is not current compensation alone but the expectancy of a *continuing* flow of income which affords status and security. Either the rate or certainty of income expected may be greater or both. The interplay of expectancy of higher income and the expectancy of a higher level of security is complex in the mind of the worker, but both are key factors in stimulating incentive.

In the study of the policies of American corporations over the past half century it has been interesting to see the steady shift to the use of arrangements for utilizing the desire for security as a basic incentive. When business concerns were small and related in stability to the fortunes of single enterprises, the employee faced the same risk as his employer. Since most employees lived close to a minimum level of security in a society accustomed to risk, the rate of time preference was high. But as corporations became permanent establishments and the economic expectations of employees rose, both the source and the desire for longer-run security expanded. It was then that employers began to recognize the value of a stable and experienced workforce and to see the advantage of programs that enhanced both regularity of employment and protection against the individual risks faced by employees.

The development of the American corporation demonstrates again the age-old interaction of organization and security. Men organize themselves into groups not only to produce more effectively but also to attain the higher level of security which greater production affords. With a higher level of security, men in groups, if properly organized and led, will produce more effectively. They do so not only because of the advantages of the subdivision of labor, but because of the built-in devices for enhancing individual incentive to attain a still higher level of security. An individual's security is no longer dependent upon the direct and often random impacts of conditions. Instead, it is influenced in large measure by the way in which his employing organization translates the risk of *corporate* enterprise in a competitive economy into a certainty that a greater individual contribution will be rewarded by a higher level of *individual* security. The challenge of enterprise and risk may stimulate the *leaders* of a corporation to greater efforts; a continuing element of risk and uncertainty unrelated to individual performance may reduce the effectiveness of the employees down the line. It is a wise leader of corporate organization who understands the difference in the impact of risk and uncertainty at the various levels of organization.

An example of a misunderstanding of the interaction of risk and incentive in the motivation of employees in large organization has been the history of profit-sharing and employee stock ownership in America. In the boom period of the 1920s the Industrial Relations Section at Princeton University made an exhaustive study of employee stock ownership. Executives were enthusiastic about this new means of encouraging worker incentive and loyalty. The stock market crash of 1929 brought the dream of "worker-capitalists" to a sudden end. The results were shattering to hundreds of thousands of workers who needed security more than ever before. Not only was the proper relation of incentive and security undermined, but both jobs and savings were lost. American executives learned the lesson that for the wage earner to be effective, incentive and security must interact within the reasonably narrow limits of the job and not in the context of the total economy. The stockholder is a very different person. His contribution to the corporation is risk capital, not day-to-day effort on the job.

In contrast to the serious shortcomings of employee stock-ownership programs for rank and file workers as a means of encouraging incentive and attaining individual security are the advantages of contributory social insurance incorporated in the Federal Old Age, Survivors, and Disability Insurance System established in 1935. With the lessons of the depression clearly in mind, the planners of the national social security program related the level of security attained by the individual contributor to his incentive as reflected in his regularity of employment and level of earnings, and not to the profits of any single employer. The social security program, within the limits and purposes of a socially oriented system, parallels the incentive-security relationship normal to the general wage economy. It reduces individual risk related to major contingencies beyond the control of the individual and at the same time encourages, through differential benefits, the exercise of incentive by the individual to attain a higher level of normal earnings.

It is a serious error to discount the noneconomic elements in the quest for security. With organization has come hierarchy and differential status. While status should properly be reflected in compensation and to some degree in greater economic security, it also provides a range of psychic satisfactions which encourage the effort to attain them. Without organization, the precise status of an individual is less apparent. With organization, whether in the armed forces, universities, churches, governments, or corporations, symbols of status that are more or less closely related to authority and responsibility are a part of the web and woof of the incentive system. The test of their effectiveness is the response of those who belong to the system. This in turn is related to the precision and integrity of the procedures by which status and its symbols are assigned.

Status, as a means of encouraging incentive, can be cheapened if it is not constantly related to the responsibilities and authority commensurate with it in a hierarchical, functioning organization. An individual promoted to a higher rank may gain an immediate satisfaction. But if others, and eventually he himself, come to see that higher status is not really a reflection of higher responsibilities, authority, or general contribution, the response which makes status an effective instrument of incentive is weakened for everyone.

The danger of excessive use of status symbols is ever present in large organizations today. The counsel of wisdom is to exercise restraint and to permit the need for designated positions of higher responsibility and authority to become clearly evident before they are established. Granting status should not be an easy way to keep people happy. Its role as an incentive for those who seek it is not diminished by making sure it remains a *by-product* of wise organizational planning. Again, in human organization, the proof of wise leadership is a broad, enduring response. Status is too valuable an instrument in sustaining the response of incentive to be cheapened by overuse.

While higher income, greater security, and higher status are the obvious instruments of the leader in encouraging incentive, they fall short of reflecting the whole complex of motivations which lead people to greater and more effective effort. Human response is enhanced by a host of stimuli, external and internal. Another fundamental art of leadership is to broaden the natural striving for self-respect, which lies deep in human personality, so that it encompasses respect for one's organization—its mission and its leadership— as well as for one's performance. The skilled craftsman has a pride in workmanship and the team player a pride in the performance of the team. There is no clearer evidence of the human nature of organization than the wide range of variation in the incentive of an organized group under conditions of strong self-respect and mutual respect compared with pro forma fulfillment of duties. Mutual respect should exist in both the vertical and the horizontal planes in organization to produce its fullest effect in motivation. The leader by his choice of personnel and by his example can go far to create the climate. Leadership, communications, and tradition combine to reinforce the psychological conditions which assure incentive.

If further evidence were needed of the importance

of noneconomic factors in enhancing incentive, one could examine the intensely human phenomenon of response to praise or criticism. One pats a horse or a dog for a job well done. (One does not pat an automobile.) The response of a human being to praise or criticism is far more complex, yet just as fundamental. In an age of mechanization and computers, there is a tendency to overlook the fact that people, despite their seeming sophistication and cynicism, remain much as they have been over the centuries.

The framing condition of the effective use of praise or criticism in leadership is sincere personal interest in the person to whom it is directed. Genuine interest in and understanding of the recipient permits one to sense the delicate balance of self-confidence and self-doubt that lies in each of us. Praise, when deserved, can go far to tip that balance. Where mutual respect exists, it can reach deep into the conscious and unconscious personality of the recipient.

Paradoxically, criticism appears to have the best effect on incentive when outward conditions are emphasized rather than inward attributes, even though the recipient may be quick to sense his own lack of success. The reason for the difference is that the essential purpose of the leader is to enhance motivation in the individual, not to weigh his faults in his presence. As long as an employee is to continue as part of the team, criticism should emphasize the better way rather than the personal fault. But praise, on the other hand, is the more effective if it is assumed to reflect the personal attributes cherished by every one of us. We want to succeed because of ourselves. If we fail, we need help in sustaining our self-respect. A leader in human organization is seeking to motivate people as they are, not to recreate them in his own image.

The leader in a large organization today faces a very different task in enhancing motivation than his counterpart in the small and simple organizations of the past. Among his possible advantages is the whole system of arrangements for the selection, training, evaluation, advancement, and compensation of employees, which are designed to undergird and enhance incentive in getting a job done well. With larger organization, the arts of supervision can be refined. Meanwhile, the wants which incentive can help fulfill have multiplied and their attractiveness has been dinned into everyone's ears. Desirable goods and services compete with various aspects of security as the rewards of greater effort.

But against these factors favorable to enhancement of incentive are those which have shifted the focus of the worker's attention from the contribution to the reward. With affluence, there has been a diminution of the ethical assumption that work is a good in itself. This principle flourished in a time when the moral discipline of religion reinforced the necessity of work as a means of individual and community survival.

Further, with the vast subdivision of labor under mass production, the sense of pride and responsibility of the worker for the quality of a whole product has been replaced in many industries and services by the measurement of effort by time and quantity. The initiative of the worker has been cribbed in by the engineer who designed and paced a highly segmented process. Specialization, mechanization, bigness, and impersonality tend to discourage human response. The effectiveness of mass production has encouraged the worker, with shorter hours of work, to focus more and more on enjoyments outside his job rather than on the satisfactions of accomplishment in the work itself.

It is not alone the methods and dimensions of productive processes which have made the enhancement of incentive more complex. The social institutions which surround those processes also play a very significant part. It can be said that the original purpose of trade union collective bargaining on the terms of employment was to counteract the employer's excessive zeal in taking advantage of the increased gains that resulted from employee incentive without sharing those gains equitably with the worker. As a result, trade unions have sought not only to obtain the best possible compensation for services rendered, but also to determine the measure of services provided, whether by time or energy expended. To do this the union has tended to standardize both. It cannot be denied that a contract of sale normally involves both the price and a designated measure of the thing sold, and the trade union, as representative of the worker, is concerned in both. The important point in relating collective bargaining to worker incentive is that a collective sale of services does not prevent the enhancement of those services in both quality and quantity *provided* there is joint agreement in these terms. With effective leadership on the part of both the management and the union, the productive process can be steadily improved to the advantage of all concerned. There are situations, however, where a union seeks to raise wages or assure continued employment by restricting output per worker. The response to such a policy is not for the employer to give up his proper role of leadership in enhancing incentive, but rather to create conditions in which enhanced productivity is truly a common advantage to all—the worker, the employer, and the consumer. The incentive and contribution of the worker in large, modern industry can be far greater than ever before, even though it is no longer, in many situations, a free response to management leadership alone.

The key words in this rather sweeping generalization on the possibility of continuing enhancement of productivity through incentive are "effective leadership"—on the part of both management and unions. In the area of incentive, there are, however, influences arising from the rapid progress of the American economy which have added greatly to the resistances which both managements and union leaders must overcome to create a climate of sustained incentive. With growing affluence, people are less acutely troubled by unfilled wants than in earlier times. There is an in-

creasing concern for leisure, whether in shorter working hours or in the pace of work within working
hours. Greater material satisfactions available through
a higher pricing of services have tended to replace the
satisfactions of accomplishment on the job. The work
ethic, traditionally supported by the Calvinist strain
in America, has become diluted by a tendency to
transfer responsibility from oneself to the large-scale
employing complex, whether a private corporation or
a government. Bigness, impersonality, specialization,
and increasing layers of supervision have all played
their part.

But the fact remains that whatever the degree of
technological advancement, it is the response of the
individual worker which counts, whether rank and
file or executive. No matter how big the organization
or how far individual assumptions in respect to responsibility shift, it will remain the challenge of
leadership—in America or anywhere else—to obtain
response from the participants in an organization,
whether a corporation or a union, favorable to its
survival and progress. A machine can be made to run
faster by remote control. A human organization increases its effectiveness through the positive response
of human beings to many influences. In the effective
human organization, the most sustained influence is
the hierarchy of leadership working through communication and tradition.

The foregoing discussion of the role of leadership
in sustaining incentive assumes that the leader is a

relatively free agent in the task of gaining response. This is the optimum condition in the typical private corporation or institution. In a trade union, a leader subject to the whims of an electorate may need to make concessions to short-run interests or to rigid conventions. But the strong union leader is able to convince his constituents of the need for a longer view.

In the limiting case of an essentially political organization, the problem of the leader in sustaining incentive becomes even more difficult. Where a political leader is chosen by the votes of his constituents, he is not the head of a hierarchical organization so far as they are concerned. When, however, he assumes executive functions in charge of public employees, he becomes the leader of a hierarchical organization. Unfortunately, the political and administrative functions imposed on the same individual can seldom be neatly separated. Civil service systems have been developed to assure the continuance of effective administration despite political change in higher leadership, but the absence of clear-cut distinction between political leadership and executive leadership has not been conducive to the highest order of incentive in government administration. In the attempt to protect the government employee, securtiy has often been emphasized at the expense of initiative.

With all the advantages and limitations faced by the leader in large organization today, the future welfare of the country depends upon the sustaining and the enhancing of incentive. Science and technology have yet to find any means of replacing human motivation. Rather science and technology have, through their contribution to bigness and affluence, strained our ability to sustain the essentially human capacity to insure dedication and enthusiasm as human organizations expand. The arts in encouraging incentive remain those of gaining response through leadership. Elaborate procedures, no matter how refined, remain but tools and not substitutes for that central human art. When leaders fail to understand this and give up their role by default, progress will slow down to a pedestrian pace and the world will succumb to universal bureaucracy.

VII

The Balancing of Response and Responsibility

THE REPEATED EMPHASIS upon the need for the leader of human organization to develop response in those who are led may suggest that the response thus gained should prevail over the convictions of the leader. Nothing is further from the truth. A leader with the attributes discussed earlier in this book could not and should not become the captive of the ebb and flow of changing opinion on the part of those less responsible than himself.

The critical contribution of the leader is rather to create response consistent with the values and purposes that *he* considers vital to his organization, as *his* mind and conscience interprets them. But his decision concerning what is essential, as well as possible, involves an understanding of the attitudes, aspirations, and motivating forces within his people. Bringing into balance the continuing pressures of individual responsibility and constituent response, whether encouraged or spontaneous, is one of the loneliest and most demanding aspects of leadership. The ability to live with the pressures arising from such interaction and to keep one's purposes clear to oneself and to others is the real test of responsible leadership in organized society.

Since leadership in human organization involves so deeply the personality of the leader, it is easier to indicate errors in approach than to explain the precise art of balancing response and responsibility. A common error is to assume that leadership is *arbitration*—the neat balancing of opinions and interests so that differences are enveloped within a clever compromise. The difficulty with this approach is that the initiative of the leader becomes diverted from attaining *his* goals. He is constantly trimming the boat. Arbitration is necessary in making bargains between equals, but a leader is *not* an equal in dealing with the members of his organization. Even in dealing with a trade union, the chief executive of a corporation is negotiating on ancillary aspects—wages and working conditions—and not on the main thrust of corporate purpose.

That an effective leader is not an arbitrator does not mean that he should not exercise the fine art of attaining a creative compromise when the compromise aids in securing mutual accommodation within the limits of sound policy as he sees it. For example, because human nature abhors suddenness, it is frequently necessary to adjust the precise timing of change. The conviction that change is necessary remains, but ideally an effective leader must judge the appropriate pace of change in advance by anticipating the response, and then he must convince people that the pace is reasonable. The history of the American railroads demonstrates the end result of passive arbitration between investors, government, and labor by railroad executives who failed to sustain leadership initiative.

If the approach that assumes that constituents are equals is unfortunate in the exercise of leadership, it is even more unfortunate to use the approach that the members of an organization are dull and docile servants. This may have worked for a while in the old days in American industry when employees were uneducated immigrants on the edge of poverty. But with the advance of education and the relative independence which trade unions and affluence have afforded, the leader who keeps his plans and purposes to himself and avoids implementing intelligent response is likely to get into trouble. It is in the nature of humankind to want information about conditions which affect their lives. If accurate information is not available, rumor fills the vacuum. The prime example of this is the scuttlebutt that permeates an army unit in time of war. To avoid leaks to the enemy, the military mind assumes that citizen-soldiers should respond only to orders when given. Anyone who has worked in a factory or office knows that rumor is not limited to the armed services. Even where higher executives understand the need to provide accurate information to gain effective response, junior officers and supervisors are prone to husband their store of "inside" knowledge.

It is therefore poor practice to try to protect the freedom to exercise the responsibilities of leadership by rigidly limiting the flow of information to which constituents can respond. Secretiveness is the disease of self-righteous dictators, and it impairs their health in time. It also impairs the morale and effectiveness of their organization, whether it is a government, a corporation, or a university. Responsible leadership requires a knowledge of response even when it is not just what the leader wants. To stem a downward flow of honest information cuts off a return flow of intelligent reaction. It may save worries for a time, but it creates a condition of isolation which leads to errors of judgment. Good intentions are not enough. And being right is not enough. The leader of an organization must also be able to move his organization to *implement* what he believes to be right.

A corollary of the secretive approach in preserving responsibility is that propaganda may be substituted for solid, relevant, day-to-day information. The proper channel for the flow of information and response within an organization is the line management supported by a closely integrated and knowledgeable technical staff, not an outside agent. With the great growth of public relations, advertising, and public opinion services, there has developed a confusion between selling soap and "selling" one's employees. If an outside agency can come in and do a better job of convincing employees that a management is wise, fair, and dynamic than the line organization of the corporation, things are in a bad way. Public opinion polling is still far too limited in effectiveness to fathom the subtleties of human attitudes and judgments, which is expected of a good foreman in daily contact with his people.

With the almost desperate need for mass markets to gain the full advantages of mass production, there has been some corrosion of the sense of responsibility for sustained quality or value in products on the part of some leaders in American industry. Lack of responsibility toward maintaining the high quality of products cannot fail, over time, to taint relations between the leader and employees. Employees are aware, long before the customer, that shoddy goods are being sold. Their response starts a downward spiral of distrust which no propaganda can reverse. The corporate tradition "let the buyer beware" becomes operative, and before long the company's industrial relations are characterized by suspicion and bad feeling. Once lost, it takes years to rebuild the mutual confidence which makes human organization truly effective.

The aberrations from the ideal in balancing responsibility and response so far discussed are more likely to occur in large, mass-production industries where huge investment requires sustained sales and profits. Leaders in nonprofit organizations are more susceptible to other kinds of errors. One is giving way to "democracy" in developing such widespread and articulate response from the members of an organization that the leader feels relieved of taking the responsibility for making tough and unpopular decisions. The leader seeks to make everyone responsible through some machinery of representation and moves only when the highest possible common factor of opinion seems to support a change. This may be called the "town meeting" syndrome.

In coping with the relatively uncomplicated problems of early New England, the town meeting served more as a policy board than an instrument of executive leadership. The members had a stake in decisions because they owned property in the town and paid taxes. They were close to the problems discussed and could accurately evaluate proposed solutions. When a job needed to be done, however, such as repairing the roof of the town hall, someone was hired to do it. The kind of organization we are dealing with took shape when the person responsible for performance, rather than policy, needed to develop a staff. The function of the town meeting itself is now served by elected town councils, corporate boards of directors, trustees, and legislatures. The executive who holds large town meetings of staff members *to determine policy* has turned his organization upside down in an attempt to introduce "democracy" at the expense of his essential authority.

If more evidence is needed to demonstrate the shortcomings of the town meeting approach, one can review the dismal history of producers' cooperatives which sprang up in America in the decades just prior to the Civil War. Even with a heavy dose of naive idealism, confusion between the function of leadership and that of response undermined the effectiveness of many noble experiments.

There is a basic distinction between a meeting of employees to receive information and a meeting of an executive's immediate staff to discuss operating policy. Both help in gaining intelligent response. Neither should infringe upon the responsibility of the chief executive to make the final decision. Large meetings, however, carry the weight of numbers, and large numbers carry influence, even when authority has been defined. A large meeting of inadequately informed persons of limited responsibility can slip into the role of a legislature, given the climate of America today. Few chief executives look forward to meetings of stockholders who do indeed have a right to be heard as well as to vote their shares of stock. Large meetings of subordinates can be even less fun. Fortunately there are other ways to obtain their views.

Experience suggests several guidelines in the development and functioning of staff groups and committees whose twofold purpose is to advise a chief executive on operating policy and to serve as an effective channel of response. Small committees are more effective than large committees. There seems some support for a norm of seven members. Such committees should meet with the executive, under his leadership and not separately. As discussed earlier, the *process* in staff consultation is more important than reaching complete consensus, since the decision making will be done essentially by the leader. It is the leader's function to encourage discussion enlightening to him, whether concerned with technical information or general response. At the same time, the sense of participation helps resolve conflicts and apprehensions.

Experience proves that the art of leadership within a small committee requires both thought and sensitivity, even though a meeting is apparently quite informal. Neither dogmatism nor disorder is likely to produce the desired results. While the leader should have thought out tentative conclusions in advance, these are best used to suggest questions rather than to give answers.

In the early stages in a group discussion of a problem, the boundaries of inquiry should be broad enough to consider the forest as well as the trees. This gains response from members of the group whose opinions may be broadly critical or nonconformist. General hunches and creative ideas are too valuable to be curtailed by a narrow approach to a problem. It is better for the group to decide what won't work after discussing the alternatives than to arrive quickly at ready-made answers.

The leader presiding over a meeting of an advisory group should avoid expressing his judgment on an issue until late in the meeting in order to sustain free-wheeling discussion by younger men. At times, it may be better to reserve judgment until a later time in order to avoid giving immediate approval to one side or the other when differences persist. Often his conclusion will draw upon both sides. It is especially desirable to avoid any counting of votes, since this emphasizes persons rather than ideas. Again, an advisory group is not a legislature. It provides response, but does not assume responsibility.

The leader's art of maintaining a balance between the pressures of individual responsibility and constituent response is deeply personal. The leader must have a mature sense of his responsibilities, developed over the years through introspective thought. At the same time he must be truly interested in people and their attitudes, ideas, and concerns, because effective organization is a distinctly human operation. It requires in its leadership a person who looks both inward and outward so that his important decisions truly take into account the whole picture.

VIII

Differentiation and Integration, Growth and Size

ONE OF THE MOST remarkable phenomena in nature is the mysterious controlling mechanism which in almost every living organism limits cellular differentiation and growth to what is compatible with efficient, functional integration. Even so huge an animal as the whale has retained its operational integrity by developing internal mechanisms, such as a heartbeat of once a minute, which maintain its vast bulk. But even with normal growth, the resulting size may lead to the extinction of the species unless the environment is suitable, as in the case of the dinosaur.

While it would be an error to transpose the findings of biology in explaining the nature of human organization, the general characteristics of living organisms are suggestive of a basic condition. Unlike a machine, living organisms face the problem of *internal* control of specialization and growth. At the same time, they must meet the test of survival through their own ability to adapt themselves in size to their total environment. Failure to control size means extinction, since nature takes no excuses. Human organizations face a similar test.

Growth in human organizations arises out of the capacity for differentiation of internal functions. This involves the functions performed by the rank and file employees, by the hierarchy of leadership, and by a complex of specialized supporting personnel. The more one studies the development of large American corporations, the more one is amazed at the extraordinary refinement of specializations in their day-to-day operations. This breaking down of functions into hundreds of interrelated parts has permitted vast increases in production. But differentiation cannot proceed without an increase in size, which permits an increasing number of specialists to perform their specific tasks in coordination with a total productive process. Mass production involves specialization not only on the assembly line but throughout the total organization which is concerned in the productive effort. Although the proliferation of specializations in manufacturing industries is the easiest to visualize, it has also proceeded at a rapid pace in government, finance, commerce, construction, and many service trades. It has brought great change in both the volume and the complexity of activity.

With a high degree of differentiation and the large size to permit it, the problems of an organization which encompasses so many interacting human parts are greatly increased. The question is: How—and how far—can the arts and artifacts of leadership be stretched to insure that large organizations retain their integrity and effectiveness?

To answer that question we must examine the impact of size and differentiation on the human beings at the lower levels of the organization, at the upper levels of leadership, and on the persons outside the organization with whom it must deal. We must also ask what is the optimum size for internal, technical effectiveness and external acceptance within the total society. When does a human organization lose its personality as such and become an amorphous collection of more or less autonomous bureaucracies? Are there limits to the size of a human organization?

It can be postulated from the first that the degree of specialization of function in human organization should be determined by the response of human beings and not by the advantages in technology and cost alone. Lack of appreciation of this principle has led to discouraged managements, turnover, absenteeism, faulty workmanship, low morale, "goofing off," and strikes. Money alone will not overcome the frustrations of the human spirit. Monotony in highly specialized performance leads not only to boredom, but to a sense of loss of personal dignity. When human response deteriorates into indifference or irritation, neither technology nor money has any magic to offset lost morale.

It has taken years for the problem of the human

response to excessive specialization to be fully understood in some of the most efficient industries in America. In part, the higher earnings which specialized mass production made possible have seemed to compensate for the frustrations on the job. Satisfaction in work has been replaced by anticipated satisfactions outside working hours. Millions, however, have gone through the cycle of earning more money, becoming accustomed to greater affluence, and then finding the satisfactions of relative affluence insufficient to overcome the growing apathy or boredom of working hours. Only in recent years have a number of large corporations come to realize that all was not well on the assembly lines or in the offices.

It is interesting to contrast this condition in mass production industry with that in small-scale agriculture, from which most industrial workers came in their own generation or in that of their fathers. On the farm, the nature of work changes from day to day and season to season. A wide variety of skills may be exercised in a single day. Subdivision of work is never so great but that the whole product is a visible reward for effort. Judgment and responsibility are directly reflected in improved results. While overall efficiency may vary widely, human satisfaction from a sense of accomplishment is ever present.

The disaffections due to specialized, repetitive work have been alleviated in some industries by the development of machines to take over such tasks. Machine switching in telephone exchanges is an example. Computers may become a substitute for many clerical functions, but operating the computers may in turn become monotonous. Some attenuation of boredom may occur when the worker alternates between repetitive jobs, but the pressures to reduce cost may militate against any methods that reduce the efficiency of sustained specialization. One common approach has been to reduce the hours of work to make dull repetitive jobs more bearable, but the fact remains that a high degree of specialization has taken satisfaction out of the way one exercises his productive ability.

Monotony is not the only sign that the progress of science and technology has outrun the ability of human beings to adapt effectively to highly differentiated tasks. While serving as an adviser to the U.S. Air Force, the author had to battle with the high command to convince them not to make military planes so complex in operation that they could not be manned effectively under adverse conditions. In the case of one design, maintenance required many different highly trained specialists. Substitution of personnel was most difficult. If one specialist were to become disabled by malaria or enemy action, the plane would lose efficiency or be grounded. The advantages of technological specialization blinded the aeronautical engineers to the distinct problems imposed by the limitations of human specialization.

In another situation, the limits of human capacity for the coordination of highly specialized tasks was tested. In a mock-up of a control center for air defense, thirty-two functions were established. Under normal load the system functioned smoothly, but when the load was steadily increased, a point was reached when all thirty-two members of the team were working at top speed with no one knowing what was happening. Again, the degree of specialization of function possible in technical design exceeded the limits in the specialization of functions in human organization. The conflict is seen in less spectacular ways in many situations where the designers of processes have failed to distinguish between the coordination of inanimate devices and the coordination of human beings.

At a higher level of management, the problem of differentiation and coordination of the human factor in organization takes on other aspects which reflect the diversity of human response to the need to integrate effort. It is only human to seek support for one's sense of worth, but it is an all-too-human weakness to upgrade the importance of one's contribution in any joint endeavor when possible. As one rises in the hierarchy of organization, contribution is easier to identify. It is also easier to exaggerate. It is almost normal for the sales manager to believe that he is at the cutting edge of profitable operations and could contribute even more if the engineering department would make fewer mistakes. The controller considers the plant manager extravagant, and the personnel director bewails the inability of foremen and office managers to develop the employees he has so carefully selected. The tendency to emphasize the importance or effectiveness of one's own contribution is normal, but the challenging task of the leader in organization is to keep uppermost the complementary and reinforcing elements of teamwork. In simple organizations, the task is made easier by the more ready visualization of results. Good blocking in a football game does not receive the cheers gained by the fullback, but the coach knows what made the play succeed.

As an organization grows in size and impersonality, differentiation in management and support functions becomes a source of strain. It is not enough for the specialized members of management to respond effectively to their common superior; they must respond effectively to each other. It is for this reason that wise managements invest more and more time and energy in bringing their functional specialists together in group discussion, level by level, as size increases. The price paid for the efficiencies of division of labor is the constant reinforcement of common understanding and mutual accommodation among the human beings who are assigned to diverse special tasks. The designer of organization charts may err just as badly as the designer of elaborate technical processes if he ignores the human reactions to differentiation of function.

It is true that in modern times factors other than ideal coordination and integration of the human participants are decisive in the determination of the size of an organizational unit. A steel mill, a railroad, or an automobile assembly plant must be related in size to the technological and economic requirements for efficient production. As any serious student of industrial relations knows, it would be a mistake to assume that the existence of such large units proves that these industries have resolved the problem of size in human organization. It has been in such industries that employees have relied most heavily upon national unions to defend their interests against a distant management. Polarization rather than community of interest has been the consequence. Perhaps it is a necessary price to pay for technological progress, but there remains a pressing challenge to seek that degree of common interest in a common mission which may still be possible.

In an effort to offset the loss of a sense of community of interest as organizations grow in size, larger organizations have sought to decentralize by establishing a number of foci of leadership around which suborganizations are built. If leadership is the key to effective organization, and if response to leadership requires some degree of personalization of that leadership, then an emphasis upon the authority and responsibility of a level of management visible to the employee should be constructive. The shift to decentralized operations and control has been widespread in many industries and businesses. There are, however, several factors involved in this measure to offset the effects of size which may cause difficulties.

The immediate problem in a move toward decentralization in which each subgroup has its own leadership is the natural desire of the central higher leadership to retain control over "critical" areas of policy. It is easy to delegate the supervision of normal operations which involve limited discretion. But when issues of companywide concern arise, it requires great restraint on the part of the central, higher leadership to avoid taking over command. As long as satisfactory costs, quality, and sales are attained, all may go well, but if a trade union threatens to strike for "unreasonable" wages or if sales decline, the central office intervenes. It may be that the local management has failed to sustain an image of fair dealing and understanding concern for its employees, or the union may be making excessive demands. Whatever the cause of a shift back to central command, the shift itself is likely to convince the affected members that they are working for a total, impersonal corporation rather than for a visible local management. It is true that the total corporation is concerned in trade union agreements which may affect costs throughout the corporation, but some way must be found to reconcile the conflict between the technical economies of large organizations and the human advantages of organizations of limited size.

There is a delicate balance between too little and too much decentralization in larger corporations. Too much local autonomy places the interests of the local management ahead of those of the total organization. In one historic case, a steel processing subsidiary of a giant American corporation followed the practice of selling its best products to outside buyers while shipping inferior products to another subsidiary of the parent company, which was obliged to accept them. This internal competition for profits led to the reorganization of the corporate structure to assure that all units were engaged in a common mission. What the local management did was understandable, but it wasn't appreciated in the home office.

Not all pressures involved in the centralization of command in large organizations are economic. When men move from subordinate to senior positions in organization, delegation does not always come easily. To those who are decisive, decision making affords a satisfaction which counseling, suggestion, and audit may not replace. It is all too easy to permit the impression to develop with subordinates that suggestions are more than *possible* lines of action, and that failure to accept them might cause their judgment to be questioned. In a study made some years ago by the Industrial Relations Section at Princeton it was found that almost all chief executives claimed that they delegated policy decisions to the officers in charge of decentralized operations more than a review of the facts indicated. The theory of decentralization was readily accepted. Its practice was subject to many exceptions, not all of them subtle.

But in human organization, the leader must gain

the response of his people, and to gain response he must know his people. His medium is a two-way chain of communication that is free of distortions caused by too great distance, too many differences in culture, tradition, attitude, or experience, and too many layers of interpretation. It is most difficult for a leader in New York to understand people in New England, Alabama, Iowa, and California, let alone Germany, Italy, or Saudi Arabia. Therefore large organizations must learn to delegate, to the fullest degree possible, those elements of leadership which make more apparent to the members of organization the image to which they should respond. To the customer, a branded product may be universally acceptable. To the employee, the management of the company is the management which affects his livelihood in Paducah, Illinois. A corporation which determines its size and structure on the basis of engineering, finance, or merchandising without regard for human response to scale has failed to understand that technologies and methods do little to change fundamental human attributes.

The recent development of conglomerate corporations combining operating units in widely diverse fields appears to be an example of a one-sided approach in organization policy. It is hard enough for the employees of a single, large, corporate unit in a single industry to respond to any clear-cut leadership image. To respond to a group of corporate officers, heavily concerned with finance and knowing little of particular industries, let alone particular groups of people, is too much to expect of normal human beings. The modern conglomerate may be a clever financial invention, but its effectiveness as an integrated human organization is still to be tested. As in the case of marriages for money, one should not expect the development of close-knit family life. Human organizations suffer when control is in the hands of people who are more concerned with technology or money than with people. The banker can do as much damage as the engineer, if, as such, he fails to understand that a human organization is not an impersonal machine.

Underlying many of the errors of Wall Street in dealing with American industry is that financiers and lawyers are prone to look upon the human constituents of ongoing organizations in somewhat the same way that a Madison Avenue advertising firm looks upon the customers for headache pills. It is assumed that the employee in Toledo or the manager in Omaha will be proud and happy to work for the great new giant complex "Universal Amalgamated" because hours of TV and radio time are used to extol the virtues of "U.A." Clever ploys sell pills, why shouldn't they create loyalty, dedication, and responsibility? The obvious answer is that the difference between two brands of headache pills, cigarettes, or even automobiles has very little effect upon human fulfillment. But the nature of the leadership under which one works for forty hours a week earning his livelihood has great influence on one's satisfactions in life.

And so, to the problems of specialization, size, and impersonality is added the problem of arrogance. What's good for "Universal Amalgamated" is good for the customer, the employee, the local manager, and the public, and we have hired the highest paid advertising firm on Madison Avenue to tell you so. One does not have to challenge the ethics of the advertising specialist to say that he is both ignorant and most casual about the day-to-day and place-by-place relationships that make a human organization worthy of respect. He can even be excused because he doesn't assume to be a leader. He is merely hired to make leaders look good. The arrogance of a management which believes that words at so much a minute can take the place of wise and consistent leadership is inexcusable. It reduces the American worker—and supervisor—to the level of a high-grade moron. Where arrogance overrides understanding, there is not much hope for effective human organization.

Clearly increasing differentiation and size make the problem of attaining integration and effectiveness in human organization increasingly difficult. Unless the capacities of leaders are correspondingly enhanced, there may well come a need to slow down, stabilize, or reduce the size of many kinds of organizations. In a country like the United States, bigness still seems a value in itself. Where human beings are involved, it can easily be an expensive mirage.

The limiting condition in growth in size is that people within organization must respond to a leadership they can sense, respect, and trust. When an organization gets too big for its leadership, it either disintegrates into amorphous subgroups or it becomes a vast impersonal bureaucracy. There is nothing to reassure us that leadership will develop sufficient in number and quality to permit the problems of size and impersonality to be swept under the desk, even the king-size desk which enlarges the ego of the president of "Universal Amalgamated."

IX

Conformity
versus Creativity

IT HAS PROBABLY become apparent by now that, in the mind of the author, at least, the quality and capacities of leadership are the critical determinants of the effectiveness of human organization. It is also a recurrent theme in this book that increasing size in human organization has put severe strains upon the capacity of leadership. These strains involve a wide range of needed attributes, but one attribute in particular appears to be almost smothered by the standardization, coordination, and centralization of control which great size usually entails. This is the attribute of creativity. With mounting size, the element of conformity grows at an accelerating rate. Creativity becomes more and more limited to the higher command and is less and less encouraged and rewarded in the lower levels of management and among rank and file employees.

It is an unfortunate paradox that when large organizations most need creativity in their higher leadership they are most handicapped in assuring its development. In a large organization a wide range of ethical, political, economic, and social concerns surcharge the climate in which top leadership operates. Yet the very perfection of a smooth-running, highly coordinated system of management stifles the exercise of creativity of those who must move up through the system into the leadership of the future. The dampening of creativity begins at the lowest ranks because processes, procedures, and policies must be standardized. It persists as individuals advance, with but limited attenuation, until, all too suddenly, the chosen leader finds himself in the lonely position of being responsible for creative solutions to problems for which computers, manuals, or past precedents provide little if any guidance.

In the study of corporate organization over many years, the author has come upon numerous instances where managements at various levels have boggled when faced with a problem which called for imagination, intuition, and creative thinking, where they could not depend upon conventional logic based on precedent alone. In one case, the company engineers had recommended that a plant employing five thousand workers should be permanently shut down because of technical inefficiencies. The company's reputation for providing security to its employees was at stake. The conflicting factors in the problem were so frustrating to executives accustomed to straightforward reasoning that they had to seek outside help. At the opposite extreme, verging on the ridiculous, the management of a local plant of a great, national corporation had to telephone Detroit to get instructions on how to get a cat off a high-tension wire. In another instance, the executives in a telephone company were so accustomed to using solid, statistical data that they failed to note that relief administrators had decided that their clients needed telephones to be advised of jobs, or that fear of burglers increasingly encouraged people to take their receivers off the phone when they were out. The tendency to follow precedent, to play safe, to depend upon statistics, to let a committee decide, to check with everyone and his brother, and to keep one's eyes in the boat appears to be part of the climate of the highly coordinated corporation. It is not a climate conducive to individual creativity.

Perhaps it is an exercise in nostalgia in an era of mass production, mass services, and mass distribution to hope that the joy of creativity will be recovered in the daily working lives of the millions. Mass production, to be profitable, requires a high degree of conformity to carefully determined standards in machine operations and human performance. There are, however, many signs of increasing restlessness, and leaders in large organizations do well to study how ordinary work can be made more interesting and more stimulating to the creative urge which resides in many people.

But the major concern in a study of human organization is how the creativity of *potential leaders* can be nurtured within a climate of conformity. To attack this problem, one must start with the factors in human personality which engender creativity of the kind most needed in organized activity. These are not too different from those in the creative person in any activity, but the emphasis may be somewhat different. An essential requirement for creativity is an inquiring mind, a persistent curiosity about things and people, particularly—in organized activity— about what makes people tick. A creative person seeks knowledge because of an emotional drive to know, not as a required exercise. But effective learning for constructive participation in leadership also requires the *orderly* analysis and accumulation of knowledge, values, attitudes, and experiences. The mind of a truly creative person may be compared to a reference library; it is filled with ideas on call for any suitable use. But this is not enough.

The critical test of a creative leader is whether he has learned to exercise his powers of intuition. This is the almost mystical ability of some human beings to rise above logic, like a jet plane leaving the runway, and to draw upon the ideas, experiences, and reactions stored deep in the mind in order to develop *new* ideas. The human mind has powers of association and combination, unconscious and conscious, which far exceed the capacity of the most advanced computer. It is not limited to quantifiable data, but ranges over qualitative intangibles which are sensed by each person in his unique way. Often a creative person cannot trace the source of a new idea which comes to his mind. The resources of a person of inquiring and orderly mind who can shift gears from logic to intuition are enormous. But he must learn to coordinate their use.

For creativity to be effective in promoting constructive change, it must be supported by other attributes. One of these is caution, the willingness to test and retest a new idea against all available evidence. This is sometimes the most difficult aspect of the process for the person of freewheeling mind. It differentiates the "idea man" from the person who gets things done. Such testing not only validates an idea's usefulness; it also provides testimony for its defense against the ever present forces of convention and conformity.

It is a further characteristic of creativity that it can be nurtured by a favorable environment, but it cannot be induced by even the most systematic training. An inquiring mind, an urge to analyze and accumulate knowledge, and, especially, a talent for using one's intuitive powers are inherent qualities that cannot be imposed from the outside. Therefore the job of any organization is to identify persons who possess these attributes and to encourage them in their use.

Creative people are more likely than most to be sensitive and introspective. Thoughtfulness, awareness of feelings, and playing with ideas are characteristics that pattern their personalities. They do not conform easily. They are not likely to be at ease with themselves or with others. If it is true that only a small fraction of the people of the world are genuinely introspective, they include a large majority of the creative people of the world.

A consideration of the qualities of creative people makes clear why organizations, and especially large organizations, face complex problems in absorbing and using the creative people they so clearly need if conformity is not to drift into dull bureaucracy. Organization requires hierarchy, specialization, and coordination. Creativity does not readily fit these requirements. It is not dependent upon age, long experience, or status for its genesis. It is likely to be free-wheeling and to suffer from excessive or prolonged specialization. Most of all, it is discouraged by an elaborate process of coordination by which a creative but unconventional idea must be screened through the minds of many less imaginative conformists.

Yet it is clearly evident that human organization, as such, must build on the momentum and tradition which experience, age, hierarchy, specialization, and coordination provide. The members of an organization must learn to submerge their personal contributions into the needs of the team. In football, a brilliant open-field runner must learn to block and tackle. In baseball, a great hitter may be called upon to bunt. In general, it can be said that organization confines and limits creativity in a vast range of functions to gain the advantages of momentum and day-to-day efficiency.

But momentum may have the wrong direction, and survival may be endangered by unwillingness to change. The creative person is needed to challenge the very forces of momentum and conformity when practices and policies are outdated. If an organization discourages creativity in its junior ranks, it comes to discount it in its higher ranks. Executives of conforming minds don't suddenly become creative as they rise higher in a corporation. Rather, they set the tone by honoring the virtues which won them promotion.

How does a large organization break the lockstep of promoting persons of conforming minds who in turn promote people like themselves? It is evident that the encouragement of creativity must start at the top and work its way down through an organization, but it is worth noting that because the effects of even one truly creative leader are usually felt far beyond the confines of the executive suite, creative people are not needed in great numbers. This is fortunate because the supply available is strictly limited. Like leaven in the loaf, it is the effect that counts.

The task involves recognition of need, recruitment, placement, nurture, constant evaluation, and intelligent advancement into more and more challenging positions in which creativity can be exercised. The objective must be the development of an upward stream within the organization of persons who can enhance their capacity for creative leadership in a structure which is under constant pressure for bureaucratic efficiency and conformity. Only by such means can a large organization assure itself of its own future leadership without dependence upon infusions at the top.

Once the need for persons of creative leadership potential is recognized, the initial step is recruitment. This may occur at any level, but one of the most favored sources is the campus. Forty years of observing the recruitment procedures of major American corporations has proved to me that conformity infiltrates recruitment even where it is assumed to be avoided. Just as the corporation itself emphasizes conformity, so the corporate recruiter comes to the college with specifications of the precise "training" or departmental program a candidate should have completed. For the recruiter, acquired knowledge is the major test, not the creative capacities of the person.

But for the creative person, knowledge is merely the means to education and not its end. The end is to gain the dynamic capacity to analyze, think, feel, develop, evaluate, express, and implement ideas—one's own ideas, not just the ideas of others. This end is attained far better in liberal, interactive education than in any program which makes the accumulation of specialized knowledge the goal. Yet the corporate recruiter avoids the most able and creative men who have had such a preparation for leadership in order to play safe with some pedestrian accountant or engineer who has had the "right" courses.

It is not surprising that a large proportion of the ablest graduates in the better liberal colleges and universities hesitate to seek positions in most large corporations. They find the law, medicine, teaching, finance, advertising, and a wide variety of smaller or individual enterprises much more appealing. But the larger corporations of the country cannot afford to lose their fair share of persons of highest potential for creative leadership at the very time that the problems of leadership are becoming more and more complex. To reverse the trend, the corporations must change. For a creative person, a high salary won't make a dull, conforming job attractive. The expectation of a liberal pension won't justify forty years in a comfortable bureaucracy.

The placement, nurture, evaluation, and advancement of a creative person in a large organization could be the subject of a long treatise on personnel management. A few basic principles can be suggested, however. First of all, persons of such talent are rare and valuable. They should be treated as such and should not be put through the wringer "for their own good." The most effective discipline for a creative person is not routine but challenge and the obligation to fulfill challenge. To put him or her through a dozen departments "to get acquainted with the business," without tough assignments and without gaining a sense of accomplishment, is to misunderstand what makes such people tick. Corporations would do well to emulate the abler university teachers who help creative persons by constantly raising their level of expected attainment and by acting as counselors in the rhythm of mastery and humility which is inherent in intellectual and emotional growth.

The key to the solution lies in the quality of supervision. The supervisor of creative people should be more a coach than a boss. He should enjoy building men even at the expense of much time and effort to explain, caution, and commend. He should learn the art of getting more done by wise and careful delegation to a younger person who can do more. Far too many big corporations have failed to develop enough good supervisors at all ranks to insure an upward flow of creative, potential leaders. In some corporations this kind of supervision is not adequately recognized and rewarded. In others, a climate of competition and personal insecurity creates so much anxiety that a supervisor is kept busy justifying himself. He has little time or inclination left to advance the progress of others. It is top leadership that sets the style and establishes the assumptions that support the development of creative persons up through the total structure. Like most good traditions, it must be the projection of wise and farsighted leadership.

Conformity and creativity are intensely human attributes. Organizations need both, but in proper balance. Conformity to a tradition of fair dealing is a great corporate asset. Conformity which smothers creativity because creativity is an unsettling, disturbing, restless attribute is a liability leading to slow decay and disaster. The interplay of these two attributes, when they are properly balanced, makes the most of the human side of organizations, large and small. Leadership must be alert to signs that indicate that the size and permanence of their organizations are increasing the difficulty of assuring balance.

X

Corporate Goals and
Individual Conscience

IN OUR ATTEMPT to understand the nature and behavior of human organizations, it is well, as in scientific analysis, to use every test one can marshal to discover the basic characteristics of the thing examined. A further test of a human organization, whether it be a corporation, an institution, a government, or a church, is, does it, *as such*, have a conscience? By conscience is meant a system of values which is embodied in the conscious or unconscious levels of personality against which attitudes, actions, and judgments are examined introspectively apart from any outside control. That individuals have a conscience is well known to every sane person. But do organizations as ongoing combinations of people develop, over time, a conscience apart from those of the individuals who are combined? Is there such a thing as a "corporate conscience"?

For the sake of clarity, a distinction should be

made between conscience and tradition. Tradition is the *vehicle* by which a vast range of habits, attitudes, standards, and expectations are carried forward through time. Among other standards of behavior, tradition may help carry forward the *outward effects* of the exercise of conscience. But the question remains, How does this exercise of conscience take place, and what is the source of its influence on behavior?

Conscience deals in values—often very subtle values—which involve so many elements of *individual* experience, background, thought, and feeling that they are essentially unique to each individual. Further, values inherent in the exercise of conscience arise from such complex associations of intangible, qualitative elements, deep in the human mind, that they cannot be fully analyzed by the individual himself, let alone be precisely expressed in definite, objective terms. Therefore, values cannot be abstracted from their source, added together among a group of individuals, and averaged to obtain a measurable *group* value.

It is extremely important to grasp this if one truly seeks the nature of human organization. Since the values inherent in individual conscience cannot be measured and added together, then how can a combined, social value develop? The answer is that there is no such thing as a common value or a corporate conscience in any substantive sense. Conscience must always develop in *individuals*, and it is the influence of individuals on corporate behavior that gives effect to conscience. Among those individuals who have, or should have, the greater influence are the leaders in organization.

The distinction between individual conscience and a "social" or "group" conscience is of the highest importance in any society. It was at the heart of centuries of conflict between adherents of two great religious traditions, Protestant and Roman Catholic. It remains a fundamental difference between democracy and communism. Does the Church or the State determine what is right, or does the individual? If the Church or State so determines, what *is* the Church or State? Does it have a corporate conscience, or does it merely enforce the expressions of the conscience of some individual person or persons, past or present? The sources that activate an individual's conscience are unique and mysterious, but this is not our concern in dealing with organization. Our concern is with those who accept the final authority of Church or State over an individual's conscience and their assumption that in some way the conscience of the leader or leaders is transmuted into a *corporate* conscience either by divine intervention or by revealed political theology. This transmutation of individual conscience into a corporate conscience has been a tragic issue of great historic proportions.

This brief excursion into religious and political history will, at least, indicate the deep significance of the question of how the manifestations of individual conscience find their way into human organization. We know that they do find their way and most certainly should. Without such a transmission, organizations have been ruthless instruments of suppression and aggrandizement. With such transmission, they have used the increased effectiveness which organization makes possible to enhance the welfare of all.

The first step in the explanation of the transmission process is to consider how individual value judgments find their way into human affairs, whether political, economic, social, or cultural. The route is by the way of an individual's *choice of alternatives* as expressed in action, no matter how complex the reasons for that choice may be. In politics, each person decides whether Candidate A or Candidate B should be elected. In economics, he decides that object X is worth more to him than object Y, with money usually one or the other item. The decision remains one of relative values, not absolute. No one can say that a famished beggar values a meal costing a dollar so much more or less than a rich man values a meal costing five dollars. No one can quantify the goodness of a man or the beauty of a sunset.

A group of people does not establish an external, objective value in absolute terms; rather the interplay of relative evaluations within each individual leads him to make a choice between alternatives. It is action based upon these individual relative choices which sets a price or wins an election. Relative evaluations of a host of individuals exercised in the arena of the political system, the market, or the community of concerned critics brings about a general preferment in elections, prices, or reputation.

And so it is with the particular kind of evaluation which concerns us here—the individual's inner determination of right or wrong in ethical or moral terms through the operation of his conscience. Conscience causes the individual to prefer one line of policy, action, or attitude over another. It is when this preference is expressed or acted upon that conscience has impact. It remains the impact of one person. He may merge the influence of conscience into a combination of other justifications for his words or actions. He may not be able, even in his own mind, to analyze and measure the constituent elements in his decision. But conscience has had its effect— through the individual—upon any community or organization in which he is active. The community or organization itself possesses no conscience apart from the individuals within it, even though the predisposition of many individuals, reinforced by *their* sense of tradition, *their* total background, or *their* innate character, might create the impression that the community or organization had itself gained an introspective conscience, a corporate soul. Regardless of any legal fiction, an organization is not a person. Nor can it have a soul.

In a study of the human nature of organizations, this conclusion is of far-reaching importance, especially when large and growing size tends increasingly to submerge the individual. As the individual becomes more and more overwhelmed by mass, an organization takes on a quality of impersonality, as if it were a great machine subject to physical laws rather than human initiative. The whole seems to become greater than the sum of its parts, not merely in economic and engineering terms, but in spiritual, ethical, and moral terms as well. This impersonality is reinforced by momentum, an assumption that any direction in which the organization moves has become more than that determined by any individual. Conformity to the direction of movement or to the current ethical climate affords the individual a sense of security which dulls anxiety, blunts the questioning mind, and assuages the individual conscience.

An appalling reflection of any sensitive student of organization is that the effect of size upon individual conscience in the evolution of large organizations suggested above slowly but persistently parallels what occurs far more rapidly in the evolution of a mob. Size, impersonality, momentum, conformity, and the suppression of individual reason and conscience are the usual attributes of that most dangerous of human combinations, a murderous mob. But one does not have to go to this extreme to sense the dangers inherent in large organization when the influence of individual conscience is dulled.

Illustrations of the effect of size on corporate behavior, when the precious ingredient of individual conscience is wanting, fill the pages of political, economic, and social history. More vivid illustrations appear in today's newspapers. A massive military establishment is so concerned in the business of crushing an opponent that it fails to control the ruthless killing of noncombatants; regulations are distorted for personal gain; clandestine intervention is extended to areas beyond established jurisdictions. A political organization uses dishonest and dishonorable means to undermine an opponent on the arrogant assumption that the end justifies the means. A large corporation sells shoddy or even dangerous products to unwitting consumers on the principle of *caveat emptor*, or permits subordinate officers to enter collusive agreements on prices while senior officers assume a role of righteous idealism, or subverts officers of government to gain special advantage at the expense of the public. The difficulty of reconciling the influences of large size and good conscience is indeed a central problem in our time.

The catalytic element which can prevent the influences of size, impersonality, momentum, and conformity inherent in large organization from restricting human dignity and fulfillment is the moral authority of a leader who is sensitive to the demands of his conscience. It is he who must encourage others to respond to their conscience—with conviction and consistency—in the functioning of the organization he leads whether it is a government, a corporation, a church, or a university. This kind of leader possesses intuitive integrity, the most precious attribute he can have. There is no substitute in law, regulation, or tradition for the conscience of the leader when issues of policy or practice involve subtle moral and ethical elements.

To permeate organization, the considerations of conscience in the leader must be communicated downward with force and persistence. Although discussion with subordinates is necessary for communication, the force of conscience in the leader must not be merged into a consensus or become the highest common factor of a group. Conscience is too inherently individualistic to be averaged out. When the chips are down the leader must work things out in lonely isolation. He is the one person who does not have to explain or argue all the constituent elements of his decisions. Even a board of directors must respect the freedom of a chief executive to follow his conscience or to resign. He must have the courage to make his convictions clear and meaningful to those he leads.

The ways in which the influence of conscience moves down through an organization parallel those of other elements of leadership. They involve the selection of personnel, two-way communication, the building of tradition, and the many other means already discussed. With issues of conscience, however, leadership is often dealing with factors in decision which are too subtle to be expressed in general, definitive terms. It is peculiarly an area in which *assumptions* must be transmitted rather than neat and tidy delimitations of what is right or wrong. It is for this reason that the communication of conscience is more effective through the personality and actions of people than through words. The worst way to transmit the influence of conscience throughout an organization, or throughout a country, is by purple language expressing high ideals which are contradicted in day-to-day acts. The credibility gap in matters of conscience is hard to fill.

Although the power of a large organization to submerge individual conscience has never been greater, the issues which should concern conscience in large organizations are far more numerous than ever before. Conscience is involved in the decision to drop an atomic bomb to end a war, or to continue a war to promote freedom at the cost of killing thousands of civilians who prefer life to a particular form of government. In a gigantic military organization, momentum, impersonality, and indoctrination may dull conscience in millions of participants in the enterprise. Vigorous activity may crowd out thought, introspection, and concern about the moral justification of a total effort. Command restricts response. It does not replace conscience either in the leader or those led.

But the effects of bigness and impersonality are not limited to military establishments. A cold war psychology has dulled the conscience of leaders in government in the administration of internal affairs. Some large corporations have sought to increase their profits through collusion with government officials. Growing financial and political power have, in these cases, corroded the influence of conscience in determining both the means and the ends in corporate activities.

It might be well in concluding this discussion of the role of conscience in human organization to distinguish between its role and that of law. Both conscience and law operate to establish standards in human behavior, but conscience is primary and internal in its influence on individual human behavior, while law remains secondary and external. The development of statutory law follows the same evolution in the arena of political activity as does price in economic activity. Both are the result of the interplay of relative individual evaluations in which conscience has influence. But the moving equilibrium of law in deciding between worthy and unworthy behavior does not relieve the individual of the need to evaluate his standards of behavior against his *own* conscience. Law is far too generalized, too insensitive to delicate nuances, and too imprecise in measuring intent to provide a sufficient rule of total behavior for the individual.

It might be argued that, with organizations, the law replaces or supersedes individual conscience. But this is only a resurrection of the straw man that there can be an intrinsic source of values in organizations apart from individuals. It projects the legal fiction of corporate "personality" developed for financial purposes in a single area of economic life to the whole substance of an essentially human entity. If to be effective organizations require leadership, communications, and tradition, and if these are impregnated with the attributes and relationships of individuals, it is difficult to believe that for one attribute alone—and that the most individual of them all—some external force takes over. Conscience has too pervasive an influence in organized activity to be replaced by law. A leader who assumes otherwise may stay out of jail, but he has failed to understand the human nature of organizations.

XI

External Influences on Organizations

IF ORGANIZATIONS are essentially human in respect to the individual foci of initiative and response which affect their behavior, then it follows that the external conditions and forces which affect individuals will also affect organizations. This may be an obvious and axiomatic conclusion, but the ramifications are not always so obvious. Organizations, unlike alarm clocks, operate differently throughout the world and throughout time because of the cultural, political, economic, and social influences upon their individual members. It is natural for people to believe that they are more insulated from environmental factors in their day-to-day business than they really are. In recent years, however, many large American corporations have become painfully aware of the manifold readjustments in established patterns of policy and operations which are necessary in developing a subsidiary overseas. To put it bluntly, what works in Indiana may grind to a halt in India.

To make clear the difference between the cultural environment in which an American corporation operates in Indiana and what it would face in developing a similar enterprise in India, some observations based on consulting experience in India may be helpful. I must strongly emphasize that in my analysis of the Indian environment as a factor influencing human organization I am not discounting in any way the positive, attractive attributes of the Indian people: their intelligence, graciousness, and gentleness; their patience under adverse conditions; their loyalty within the family and to their respected leaders; or a personal style of life and thought which only long tradition can develop. I am discussing, rather, particular human attributes which would affect the development of an industrial plant in rural India in ways quite different from a similar enterprise in rural Indiana. By such an extreme comparison, the pervasive effect of environment upon leadership and response within human organization can be more clearly set forth.

In India, there is an age-old tradition which emphasizes the command approach to leadership. India has been under the control of ruling classes for centuries, and the inheritance of the Mughal conquerors still lies deep within millions of people. This cannot but affect the attitude of the leader in India, where the imperative to elicit response from a self-determined constituency is lacking. Further, the philosophic fatalism of those led encourages a passive acceptance of status and conditions except in times of great mass emotion. "If I am poor, the gods intended me to be poor. I am not really responsible for my condition." This is accompanied by a static sense of time moving through a rhythm of annual cycles of sowing and harvesting for the community and a life cycle of birth, maturing, and death for the individual. The concept of progress, both individual or social, is something relatively new in a civilization which has seen centuries pass with little change in status for hundreds of millions.

In such a culture there is respect for elders and for group decision. There is a tendency to avoid individual responsibility and individual risk. "Why be the first to change and lose?" This has long led toward leveling the individual to the common status of the group. Differential returns for differential contribution through unusual ability or effort are questioned. These attitudes are serious obstacles to the development of differential standards in selection, wage and salary levels, responsibility, and promotion.

With this emphasis upon preserving a status that has been conferred by the accident of birth rather than seeking to advance oneself by individual effort, there is a persistent distrust among individuals and among groups of different caste, religion, or level of status, either higher or lower. Distrust creates resistance to sharing authority with others, especially those of lower status. This lack of trust, which affects both the leader and those led, discourages the building of hierarchical organization.

Perhaps most frustrating to an American executive seeking to organize an industrial enterprise in India is the predisposition of a people for whom traditions give security, and for whom time is endless, to substitute long-continued discussion for decision and action, especially where change is involved. In an Indian village council of elders, an issue may be discussed for years with apparent satisfaction. Action is quite another matter.

The American assumption that discussion should lead to decision and action is characteristic of a frontier, progressive society made up of people who left their homes to make their fortunes. Our culture emphasizes individual responsibility, individual decision, and a blending of reason and emotion into an urge to act. Further, we assume that others will join with us in acting for the common good of all. It is in this mutual accommodation to convert ideas into action that the genesis of effective organization occurs. An essential ingredient in the process is the willingness to accept leadership, to which we will respond not because the leader asks us to but because it is in our own best interests. It is not too great a simplification to say that in India, discussion usually leads to further discussion, whereas in Indiana, discussion normally leads to action—in organized cooperation with others where appropriate. Such habits of mind run deep in any culture and, influencing the individual, are bound to influence human organization.

India is only one of scores of countries and regions throughout the world where obvious and deeply entrenched cultural factors create serious problems in the development of the large-scale, integrated organizations to which Americans have become accustomed. But there are many countries far more like our own in cultural tradition where subtle differences in customs, attitudes, and aspirations exist and must be understood and respected if organizations are to function effectively. Such differences may help or hinder the leader gain favorable response in terms of incentive, responsibility, and cooperation. They include such factors as class, race, religion, family interest, respect for status and authority, ambition, thrift, and governmental intervention. Without assessing each impact or assuming that any country is free of obstacles or favored with ideal conditions, it is enough to know that external cultural environment influences how human organizations act because they are human and not like alarm clocks. Nations vary widely in all aspects, but different peoples with similar cultural characteristics react differently to new influences and construct different social patterns. No one a hundred years ago could have visualized the contrast in the progress of large-scale organization represented in two great Asiatic nations today, Japan and India.

It is also true that changing conditions within a

single culture have their influence on human organization. Some trends within America may be suggestive. An increasing desire for the material symbols of status is now in conflict with our traditional social egalitarianism. The president of the company drives to work in his Cadillac and parks it in his reserved space. But on entering the building, he greets everyone from the guard at the door to the vice president down the hall by his first name. As an unconscious reaction against the impersonality which comes with size, the participants of large organization seem to exaggerate the egalitarian symbols of informality. But the surface informality which pervades our American culture does not attenuate the insistent pressure in large organization to make status a powerful instrument for incentive. To get ahead in material terms is still a strong urge for most Americans. Proofs of status, both on the job and elsewhere, are pervasive. Never before have there been so many institutional symbols of prestige—great new buildings topped by spacious executive suites paneled in rare woods, attentive aides, private planes, expense accounts.

It might be hoped that the American trend toward informality would strengthen the sensitivity of leaders to the human nature of organizations, no matter how large and complex they may be. But the countertrend toward increasing emphasis upon differential status and upon competition to gain status in great hierarchical structures may neutralize this humanizing influence.

The essence of leadership in organization is responsibility, and differences in responsibility involve differences in status which a show of egalitarian informality cannot disguise. If differential status comes to be reflected more and more in material symbols and less and less in concern for people, organizations will lose a vital cohesive force. Effective human organizations, no matter how large, must be built and held together by the persistent interaction of leadership and response, not by the superficial symbols of assumed equality or the exaggerated symbols of status. In America, our cultural predisposition to egalitarianism on the one hand and for material success on the other may come some day to create a condition of "organizational schizophrenia."

There are many examples of the effects of these two cultural patterns in the operation of American organization. One is the great proliferation of titles in many corporations, banks, government departments, and universities. It would be difficult to imagine a title which is not being used today as a status symbol to satisfy the competitive urge for distinction. Further, the differential accoutrements of status have become equally refined, including not only the size and location of a person's office, but the decor, size of desk, and the presence of a vacuum water bottle. But with all this, the rules of the game require an appearance of democratic camaraderie until someone fails to enhance the profits of the company. Then the difficult problem arises: How do you fire dear old Joe, or send him to Siberia, so that some young comer can take over his nice office? It is then that old Joe might, retrospectively, have preferred responsible and understanding leadership to egalitarian good fellowship, and a sense of guided accomplishment to the passing symbols of status.

The discussion of incentive indicated the problems which arise when affluence, specialization, and boredom corrode the normal urge to work to get ahead. The dichotomy between egalitarianism and competition for material symbols of status is centered in the higher levels of organization where differentials are clearly apparent. For the great rank and file, an egalitarian climate is normal, and economic progress is determined more by conditions and efforts common to the group than by individual initiative. The trade union emphasizes brotherhood and better wages and hours for all through collective action. As a democratic organization, the trade union must reflect the interests and concerns of a majority of its members.

In the cultural climate of America today the concern of millions of rank and file workers in specialized and boring jobs is for more leisure, more coffee breaks, and shorter hours. Relative affluence affords attractive ways of enjoying leisure. There is a tendency on the part of those who have not studied the conditions surrounding rank and file employment today to bemoan the loss of a work ethic and assume that the fault lies largely in the corrosion of the moral and religious undergirding of our society. Whatever the merit of such a view, it greatly oversimplifies the problem. The urge to work, to accomplish results, and to gain recognition, respect, and return for work done is very deep in human nature. It is, however, affected by the total environment to which the worker responds.

There needs to be far more study of how the total environment of work in American factories, service trades, offices, and government activities can be improved. Pay alone cannot offset dullness, monotony, lack of participation, disinterest on the part of management, or lack of individually recognizable accomplishment. Work is not alone what a person does to a product or in performing a service. It is also, in a very positive way, what it does to himself and his sense of well-being in the process.

To make this concept of the psychology of work more understandable, it is helpful to examine the effects of the absence of work. It is common knowledge that a sudden shift from sustained work to unalloyed leisure on retirement involves psychological adjustments which many men fail to make. After a few weeks of "vacation," the retiree suddenly realizes that he is no longer under sail, and time hangs heavy. A serious effect of layoff or continued unemployment is the loss of the sense of self-approval which work affords. If he is wise he finds some sort of work to satisfy his instinctive want of accomplishment. Many retired people are using their leisure to work on new projects which satisfy them either in the material results afforded or in the services rendered to others.

If we are to sustain incentive in human organization, which is vital to its welfare, we cannot disregard the cultural influences which affect incentive. Human beings require a changing *balance* of accomplishment through work and recreation through leisure, and the problem of attaining such a balance is too important to be left to engineers, accountants, and stockholders. The planning and execution of a design for a satisfying way of life in an age of science and technology is one of the most challenging tasks for the leadership of large organizations. There will need to be some shifts in emphasis from how the customer likes the product to how the worker likes to produce it—unlike the ancient Greeks, we cannot sustain a culture on the backs of unwilling slaves. The extension of interest on the part of some American trade unions from wages and hours to the way in which work is done suggests the need for serious joint study in many industries.

Another cultural change that has affected human organization in America is the steadily rising level of education attained by the rank and file of American wage earners. An immigrant steel worker or an automobile assembler fresh off a southern tenant farm was a far more malleable person than today's high school graduate with ideas of his own. The number of workers who have been exposed to the intellectual and social influences of a college campus is increasing steadily. At the same time that increased education enhances the capacity of many to progress beyond the lower ranks in industry, it will also broaden the expectations of the large group for whom higher positions don't exist. Since the economy cannot absorb more than a limited number of leaders, supervisors, and staff specialists, the working life of those led must afford more satisfactions of mind and spirit than it has before.

It is foolish to assume that, for an educated person, four days of boring repetitive work can be offset by three days of leisure. Nor is money alone the answer. Since the upward trend in education can hardly be reversed in a democratic country, the solution must be found in a parallel upgrading of the total arrangements of work to adjust them to the needs of a more educated citizenry. The kinds of adjustment will vary widely in the vast complex of industry and services that give employment to eighty million people, but some areas will recur often: less specialization of task, participation in planning, rotation of function, and understanding supervision. Those responsible for leadership must retain responsibility, but that responsibility must include enhancing the satisfactions of educated persons who work under their supervision.

Within the last two decades Americans have increasingly resorted to advocacy in dealing with political, economic, and social problems rather than seeking constructive compromise under trusted leadership. Where people are unhappy in their work—or in the lack of it—the bitterness reaches into labor relations, race relations, community affairs, and politics at all levels. The needed cohesiveness for effective organization is impaired by the accentuation of differing interests by advocates who assume to represent those interests.

The most fertile source of disaffection is not where everyone faces a common condition of work or life, but rather where there is a sense of *relative* deprivation on the part of some. In America, the black minorities in urban ghettos compare their lives with suburban whites. In Northern Ireland, discrimination in hiring or category of work as between Catholics and Protestants has led to war. There is no wish to disregard the many other causes of conflict and social discontent, which any forward-looking society must deal with in basic, direct ways, but it has been demonstrated time and again that when people have satisfying work and are reasonably compensated, they are more reasonable about their demands.

The specification of *satisfying* work is significant, not the pay alone. In the Depression of the 1930s, large numbers of unemployed people were given make-work jobs. In many instances such work further reduced morale. Instead of the satisfaction of *earning* one's livelihood by self-respecting accomplishment, the performance of an assignment became a work-test for relief. Fortunately, from this experience, the country turned to unemployment insurance as a more constructive approach to the problem. It is fair to state that this approach, if introduced years earlier, would have prevented the bitter advocacy illustrated by the sit-in strikes of the period.

It would be a serious sin of omission to close this discussion of the external influences upon organizations without some reference to the positive influence of the expanding and constructive efforts of corporate leaders in America to improve social conditions in their communities. With growing size and increasing economic impact on the one hand, and an educated citizenry increasingly sensitive to human needs and rights on the other, the larger corporations in America can no longer assume a negative, passive, or grudging attitude toward participation in the solution of problems created by industrialization, urbanization, and population growth. Such participation is a matter to be determined not by legal charters or immediate economic interests but, rather, by the individual consciences, understanding, and judgment of the leaders of each corporation. This is, again, because organizations are essentially human and not merely legal or economic mechanisms. There is much evidence in the experience of progressive corporations to justify the conclusion that sensitivity to social obligation is a sign of the maturity of organizations as well as individuals.

Not only does the participation by the leadership of a corporation in the solution of community problems enhance the *public* image of the corporation; it also deepens concern and respect for human obligation *within* the organization. Wholesome attitudes toward people and their problems cannot be neatly confined to one area and not be extended to another. The outside activities of officers, which are readily understood and commended by employees distant in level and place, help project the intangible qualities of leadership. Internal, day-to-day decisions by the same executives may seem but the grist of the mill. The fact that a president sees fit to lead a United Fund drive in New York goes far to set a pattern for the local manager in Peoria.

If a further justification is needed for external activities on the part of corporate leaders, it can be argued that larger organizations have absorbed too much of the leadership talent of America to restrict its use to internal interests alone. If such organizations want to sustain and, even more, to contribute to the flow of high talent up through the long and demanding road to corporate leadership, they should recognize that the talented young people of today have broader concerns than their fathers and grandfathers.

The areas in which organizations have extended their influence for good outside their normal operations have multiplied rapidly in recent years. It is sufficient to mention participation in the improvement of educational and employment opportunities for the disadvantaged; in community planning, including housing, transportation, control of pollution, and improvement of the general environment; improved administration of schools and colleges; in the improvement of health and a wide range of social services; and in the enhancement of the cultural resources of the community and the nation.

This is an almost overwhelming range of possible involvements. Of course, each organization, to survive and grow, must sustain its primary mission. Just how far and in what direction to go beyond fulfillment of this basic obligation is for the leadership of each organization to decide on the basis of individual conscience, understanding, and judgment within that leadership, and especially within the mind of the top leader. It is increasingly clear, however, that the American people no longer question the principle that corporations, as human organizations, must respond sensitively to social obligation. In the face of the many demands upon them, the leaders of corporations must decide how best they can respond in the light of their particular situation.

The external influences upon organization discussed in this chapter are but illustrations of the wide spectrum of factors which affect an essentially human association of people brought together to perform a function. It is imprecise to pass them off as broadly "social" influences. Their impact is upon individuals *within* the organization who in turn affect the pattern, effectiveness, and survival of the organization. They are a part of the total environment, internal and external, in which leadership must strive to gain response in the accomplishment of corporate purpose. The more the leader of organization understands the human beings within it and the environment in which they live and work, the greater the contribution he can make to his organization and to the society in which it functions.

XII

Education for Leadership in Organization

IN THE PRECEDING discussion of the nature of human organization, the emphasis has been so often placed upon the attributes and role of the leader at the higher levels of organization that it seems appropriate to conclude with a consideration of the means of preparing a leader for his demanding role. Shelves are filled with books and manuals on the training of potential executives. Many of them assume that the executive will control a smooth-running machine for which he will need specialized managerial skills and decision-making abilities based upon the analysis of quantitative data. With our emphasis upon the fundamentally *human* nature of organization, it seems essential to be more concerned with the person who uses such managerial skills and techniques than with these supporting instruments. If the leader as a *human being* is of first importance in his role in organization, then his education as a whole person is more significant than his training in specific methods.

The role of the leader as such, and not merely as a supervisor of technical operations, is to gain effective response from those he leads. He will, throughout life, face a wide variety of people, conditions, and problems. The methods he uses will also vary widely since they should involve sensitive response. But his individual resources—his human understanding, introspection, intuitive integrity, his sense of responsibility, his courage and decisiveness, his desire for accomplishment, and his personal style—are unique, ever present factors in his effectiveness. They develop from youth throughout life and are basic to whatever methods he may use to gain response. It can be argued, therefore, that that part of education, whether formal or not, which enhances these basic factors is more central to his preparation for leadership than specific training in the ancillary techniques of management.

I am fully aware that my position runs counter to two basic assumptions held by many in American higher education today. The first is that education can be knowledge-centered rather than man-centered. The second is that professional education, peculiarly, should deal almost exclusively with specialized knowledge and specialized techniques related to the practice of the particular profession. I am convinced after a half century of experience that the first assumption—that education at the college level is primarily an accumulation of knowledge—is one of the most serious obstacles to the improvement of higher education in America. As to the second assumption, I am convinced, after long study of leadership in American organizations, that overspecialization in professional training built upon a knowledge-centered college program has reduced rather than increased the total effectiveness of leadership.

Men and women may become leaders despite their formal education. But a democracy requires far more leaders, and better ones, than any other political, economic, or social system. It seems worthwhile, therefore, to consider the kind of education best suited to develop the capacity for leadership in the vast range of human organizations which together determine the character of our society.

It may be necessary to remind the reader that we are considering education for *leadership* and not necessarily the education of the millions of persons who are not called upon to exercise this demanding function. Among the latter are not only the rank and file of those who are led, but also the solo specialists who depend upon others to frame their political and economic lives. For them, knowledge, skills, and techniques may be sufficient. Unfortunately, in America, with its emphasis upon the mastery of special knowledge, there is a tendency in some professions to assume the prerogatives of leadership with an arrogant disregard of its demanding obligations. A broader and more fundamental kind of education might have encouraged a more humble and understanding attitude.

There is no wish to discount the great need for knowledge and skills in the leader who *has* developed the basic attributes emphasized throughout this book. The core of my argument is that, in the leader, specialized knowledge and skills are a part of the super-structure of his total makeup, not the foundation. It is in the relative emphasis and the timing in the educational process that the distinction becomes clear.

In the formal education of a young person with leadership potential there appears to be a rhythm of (a) education in conformity and (b) education in creativity. The terms "conformity" and "creativity" are intended to sharpen the contrast between (a) learning the externally established skills and knowledge which prepare young people for civilized living and (b) acquiring the capacity as an individual to react with intelligence and feeling as knowledge and experience accumulate. In the early years of education the emphasis is upon language, mathematics, science, and a knowledge of one's culture. But as college education nears and proceeds, this approach in which one conforms to what is known and accepted should shift increasingly to that of encouraging the individual to create for himself a life-long resource of capacities for analysis, evaluation, judgment, belief, understanding, and feeling. The change to professional education should repeat the cycle, providing education in conformity in the essential knowledge and techniques of a profession, again followed by a period that stresses individualized, creative activity stimulated by the more specialized knowledge and experience one has gained.

It is essential in the whole process of education that neither conformity nor creativity crowd out the other, although the emphasis changes. A set problem in arithmetic must be solved correctly, and an original thesis must be in understandable prose. But it is in the period of education when there is freedom to inquire and interact within a community of fellow inquirers that the attributes of leadership, as opposed to those of specialized knowledge and skills, are most likely to be fostered. This is the period of *liberal* education which a good college should provide. Unfortunately some colleges do not concern themselves with truly liberal education, and many effective leaders have had to gain it for themselves.

What pattern of liberal education for leadership should the college years provide? Since it is intended to help students respond to their fellow men and to those conditions and factors which influence men, it should be man-centered and not knowledge-centered. In liberal education, knowledge is a means of education, not its end. The end is the enhancement of the powers of the individual to live a fruitful, effective life and to help others do so. It is for this reason that this kind of education is most suited to the development of leaders.

Liberal education is in itself an experience in leadership and response. The teacher and all the authors of the books studied are effective as "leaders" in the search for truth only as they obtain an interactive response from the student. There is an old rule in liberal education that there is no impression without expression. The responsive interaction of student and teacher, as well as of student and fellow student, is vital not only for clear understanding of knowledge, but for the development of an integrated system of values, intuitive insights, attitudes, intellectual habits, and judgments in the student. This is the function of liberal education that justifies the statement that, in such education, knowledge is a means rather than the end. But it is true that enlightening interaction is most likely to occur when the student has a growing interest in the area of knowledge studied. It is well, therefore, to suggest the fields of knowledge which seem most appropriate in the interactive, liberal education of a potential leader in a rapidly changing world.

In such a world, a potential leader should develop a sense of history, that the future grows out of the past. This includes the ability, through the study of many periods and areas of history—cultural, political, and social—to sense and understand the basic factors in change which often lie beneath the surface, but which gain momentum over time. The sensitive and analytical mind learns to assess the forces toward change before they become obvious. The gradual building of a sense of history, an urge to seek causes, and a willingness to avoid comfortable complacency in interpreting the present in terms of today alone are valuable attainments in a potential leader.

A sense of history helps one to gain perspective and to see the vital distinction between the conservation of a principle and a change in the appropriate method to conserve that principle. Conservatism without a sense of history is rigid and brittle. Conservatism in respect to tested principles, but with a sense of history and of evolutionary change, is the bulwark of lasting organization. Its source must be in the leadership of an organization. Such leadership assumes change and anticipates the conditions and requirements involved in adjusting to it.

The development in the potential leader of a sensitive understanding of human response, both individual and group, may be encouraged in many ways. More effective than a course in psychology is involvement in and appreciation of the great works of literature in which men, more inspired than any psychologist, have interpreted the response of all kinds of people to a vast range of conditions and events. The study of literature enhances, by thousands of unconsciously stored memories, one's ability to anticipate the responses and reactions of people.

The capacity to reach out from one's self into the mind and emotions of others is a basic requirement for leadership. No one, for example, should have authority over others without a keen sense of tragedy. Tragedy, like a submerged reef, lies beneath the surface in all human experience. A leader must understand its impact and how it can be softened to avoid loss of confidence and motivation in himself and in others. Apart from the personal experiencing of tragedy, there is no better way to gain this understanding than by reading Shakespeare under the guidance of an inspired teacher. Indeed, reading illuminates and objectifies personal experience.

The powers of analysis and the orderly accumulation of knowledge can be gained in many disciplines. The essential goal, whatever the subject, is to resolve the bits and pieces of knowledge into wisdom—an ability to discern general principles which stand the test of time. But the process is best learned at the fundamental levels of well-established disciplines, not in the review of merely descriptive material. The true meaning of "discipline" in higher education is the power to resolve all available and relevant resources, consciously and unconsciously, into the best possible determination of truth. The experience gained in the study of philosophy, the humanities, the social studies, or fundamental science is a valuable resource for the person who must perform the same function in leadership.

If communication is organization in action, liberal education should emphasize, in the preparation of the leader, the whole range of the communicative arts, through oral discussion, through exact and lucid writing, and by every art form to which people respond. A leader may not need to be an orator, author, poet, actor, or musician, but he should have some sense of how the best of these communicate ideas and emotions. The complexities of oral and written communication have been discussed earlier. The seeking of mastery is a life-long effort. It is helped by both reading and exercise, not alone in one's own language, but in others, in order to sense the distinction between words and ideas. There is no better time to develop the fine art of communication than in the years of concentrated liberal education when both guidance and a rich spectrum of exciting material are at hand.

The most essential requirements in the development of a leader are those most difficult to program in any formal manner in liberal education. They are, rather, gained in the general climate of such education. They include intellectual and moral integrity, the urge to learn and understand, humility despite growing mastery, a sense of total responsibility, and a dedication to excellence. These are the precious by-products of association with the great minds of the past and with teachers and fellow students who are engaged in seeking truth. Many of these virtues take root in childhood, but the period of liberal education in college helps to confirm and refine them in a free and intensely invigorating environment.

There can be no precise proof of what liberal education contributes to a person's integrity, humility, or dedication to excellence. The results are deep within the person who has been exposed to the experience, ever maturing as years pass. In liberal education, the product is a person, not his knowledge alone. Hopefully, it is a person better qualified to lead than if he had missed its catalytic influences.

And so, in this discussion of the human nature of organization, we end where we began, on the focal human being, the leader. And within the leader, we end where we began—with the intangible, subjective elements of his personality. In view of the mounting problems of the world today, there has never been a greater need for leaders with human understanding, a capacity for introspection, intuitive integrity, a sense of total responsibility, courage, decisiveness, a desire for accomplishment, and a personal style which will project these qualities through the increasing smog of bigness and mechanistic bureaucracy.

DATE DUE

NOV 1 0 '78			
OCT 1 8 1990			

58597